Emotional Intelligence

The art of reading people, managing your emotions, and building self-confidence. Learn how to stop overthinking, overcome negativity, raise EQ, and improve emotional agility

This Book Include:

1 - How to analyze people

2 – Cognitive behavioral Therapy made simple

Peter Rajon

JOIN OUR SUPPORT GROUP

To increase the value you receive from this book, I strongly recommend you and strongly encourage you to be part of our tight-knit and active community on Facebook.

Here you will be able to connect and share with like-minded people who want to improve themselves or overcome their problems

Making this journey alone is not recommended, and this can be an excellent network for you.

It would be nice to connect with you there,

Peter Rajon

>> Click here to join our Self-Help group <<

Index

CHAPTER 8 138

Art of Persuasion and Influencing People

CHAPTER 9 151

HOW TO ANALYZE PEOPLE

The simple guide on understanding the art of reading people, human behavior, personality types, the power of body language, and how to influence others.

Peter Rajon

This eBook, Book is provided with the sole purpose of providing relevant information on a specific topic for which every reasonable effort has been made to ensure that it is both accurate and reasonable. Nevertheless, by purchasing this eBook, you consent to the fact that the author, as well as the publisher, are in no way experts on the topics contained herein, regardless of any claims as such that may be made within. As such, any suggestions or recommendations that are made within are done so purely for entertainment value. It is recommended that you always consult a professional prior to undertaking any of the advice or techniques discussed within.

This is a legally binding declaration that is considered both valid and fair by both the Committee of Publishers Association and the American Bar Association and should be considered as legally binding within the United States.

The reproduction, transmission, and duplication of any of the content found herein, including any specific or extended information will be done as an illegal act regardless of the end form the information ultimately takes. This includes copied versions of the work, both physical, digital, and audio unless the express consent of the Publisher is provided beforehand. Any additional rights reserved.

Furthermore, the information that can be found within the pages described forthwith shall be considered both accurate and truthful when it comes to the recounting of facts. As such, any use, correct or incorrect, of the provided information will render the Publisher free of responsibility as to the actions taken outside of their direct purview. Regardless, there are zero scenarios where the original author or the Publisher can be deemed liable in any fashion for any damages or hardships that may result from any of the information discussed herein.

The book HOW TO ANALYZE PEOPLE: The simple guide on understanding the art of reading people, human behavior, personality types, the power of body language, and how to influence others, is reprinted by permission.

INTRODUCTION

Congratulations on purchasing How to Analyze People and Understand the Human Mind and thank you for doing so.

The following chapters will discuss the art of reading the human mind and peeking into their personality in a subtly effective way. The human personality is like a jigsaw puzzle; it has a complete set pattern to be followed. The puzzle should be put together by joining the missing pieces in such a way that each piece is fitted perfectly into its corresponding place. The set-provided pattern acts as a photo image or a prompt to match the pieces accordingly, almost like a comprehensive analysis. This book helps you better understand the way of performing that analysis. The person analyzing the human personality may realize that the behavior patterns, the motivational factors, the color preferences, the body language, and the verbal communication styles, etc. are all important indicators of an individual's personality. When you are learning the art of behavioral analysis and speed-reading people, you should be able to understand that observation is vital to analyzing people. It is key to opening the door of hidden character traits, behaviors, and emotions that were quite unnoticed before due to a lack of tactful observation. To be able to perceive your subject's personality and speed-read his mind, you should able to adopt techniques that will help you not only better capable of understanding his intentions, words, and actions, but also let you influence his mind. In this book, there are 33 actionable techniques mentioned that can be learned and practiced systematically in the span of just 5 weeks. Let's learn them! There are plenty of books on this subject on the market, thanks again for choosing this one! Every effort was made to ensure it is full of as much useful information as possible, and please enjoy it!

CHAPTER 1

IMPORTANCE OF ANALYZING PEOPLE AND UNDERSTANDING THE HUMAN MIND

P eople often think that the easiest way to understand the human mind is by studying your own mind. However, the fact is that the human mind is a complex bundle of entangled nerves and feelings. Even if it is your own mind, you have to delve deeper and work harder to understand the underlying intricacies of your cognition. On the other hand, when it comes to understanding someone else's mind, the process requires seemingly difficult yet systematically easy techniques to follow, which can eventually lead to an understandable pattern of human mind analysis.

Humans are interesting beings with astonishing mind powers, functioning abilities, and responses. The more we dig, the more we come up with unveiled facts and layers of the mind. The memories, the past experiences, the learned lessons, the emotional chaos, the relational feelings, and each and every bit of life's practicalities are etched on the mind.

No matter what the circumstances are and who the confronter of these circumstances is, the mind has a response to each particular stimulus that is presented by the situation at hand. This sort of reactivity makes the human mind prone to dynamic changes and psychological conditioning. It also makes a person unique from his other contemporaries. The variable quality of the human mind is quite similar to how unique each person's impressions are from the other. From afar, each of them may seem to have more or less the same nose, pair of eyes, ears, and the same number of fingers. However, when one observes carefully and comes to have a closer look, the uniqueness unfolds.

Experts suggest that human mental structures are different from each other in their wiring and conditioning because there are several factors influencing humans. People shape their minds according to the factors related to their environment, culture, society, work ethics, and tradition. To understand the workings of people's minds, we must first get to know these influential factors ranging from psychological, emotional, physical, and moral domains to professional, relational, lingual, and societal aspects.

Human society is a combination of differentially, unique beings. They cohabit, interact, and build up relationships. There is always a curious aspect lingering under the initiative of interaction. The interaction becomes fun when it stoops to the same level and frequency of mental chemistry. The communication at both ends become fluent, less awkward, and more interesting. On the other hand, if the communicators are not in sync due to their opinion differences or lack of familiarity with each other, or difference in mental levels, the interaction would be quite awkward and boring. This usually happens when practical strangers from different backgrounds come in contact and try to interact without properly knowing each other's mindset. Contrarily, without interaction, it would have been difficult to know a person and analyze the human mind.

When it comes to human behavioral analysis, it means to consider a person as your subject of study. It may sound quite mechanical and materialistic, but rest assured that there are more feelings involved in this than you imagine. Every single bit of the brain is an emotional rollercoaster of feelings and thoughts.

The mind works the way it feels. - I. F.

To survive in this society and to do it successfully, one must possess an awareness of not just his own self but the people he lives with and meet frequently or might have a chance to meet in the future. Awareness is such a deep, enlightening concept. If we study it, we understand that it is not just an internal process; instead, it involves the internal sensory perception and an external acquisition of information. This information coming from external via internal sensory perceptive organs acting as windows of awareness gets to be interpreted by cognitive receptors and output as comprehensive knowledge.

How gratifying would that be if, in this huge world, peace, love, and mutual understanding could prevail due to the avoidance of possible conflicts, clash of opinions, antagonism, and several misunderstandings? This avoidance can be possible by gaining not only self-awareness but also people's awareness. Howard Gardiner has named this sort of awareness as being people smart. Many would name it as emotional intelligence, too. The concept of EQ, however, will be discussed in detail in the later chapter of this book. For now, let us imagine how people must become intelligent in analyzing themselves and their fellow beings to make this world more livable. The world could become a happy place of friendly dwellers if all sorts of conflicts could be resolved due to being aware of the strengths and shortcomings of your fellows, their thoughts and actions, and of their motives and intentions. This is in no way being judgmental; it is readily aware of how you or any other person may behave in a given situation. It is possible; it is achievable. The term utopia would not be just for an imaginary concept. Similarly, people would be eager to sort out their potential problems and issues on the basis of this state of harmony and understanding. This may seem quite a far-fetched notion, but at least we can start from somewhere.

"Little drops of rain can make the mighty ocean." When Julia Abigail Fletcher Carney wrote this amazingly true verse, she actually tried to convey the importance of small efforts made by each living individual which can eventually combine together to make a noticeable difference.

Experts believe that the possibility to bring a change begins with an effort to alter the dynamics of the world you live or the action frame of your everyday life. You may have heard the phrase "thinking outside the box." Let us alter it a bit for you by phrasing it as tailor the box to fit the thought in. This happens when you are constantly on the move, thinking solutions, analyzing the work patterns, and thinking behaviors. This happens when you realize how crucial it is to interpret what people think, say, and do. This happens when how they behave starts to influence you as well, whether in the short run or long run eventually. This realization takes you on the route to discovering the secrets of the human mind, unearthing the complex thoughts, and understanding the behavioral patterns that not only shape an individual's mental schemas but also collectively form a public mindset, influencing the overall demographics. The mental schemes are not a set criterion box. They are not static; they are not fixed. There is always some sort of accommodation or assimilation taking place. You should understand the structural dynamics and the logical changes that are taking place in the box of your mind and be able to tailor that box according to these changes.

Suppose you meet a person who is a practical stranger to you, what can you do to break the ice in between? How will you start a conversation? Which topic will you choose? These questions are all quite dynamic in nature. Just like the dynamic nature of the human mind, human interactions are also quite unique from person to person. Maybe you are stuck with a person in a train's compartment for a long journey spanning hours. The silence, although speaks a lot when no one is speaking, becomes overwhelmingly burdensome after a while. That person is observing you by throwing subtle glances your way. You are also doing the same when he is not doing it. How do you think your glances will help you analyze him? The results may vary according to the techniques you are keeping in mind while analyzing him. What does his posture tell you? What are his facial expressions while being silent? Does he seem expressive enough? Does he seem like a stoic person? If he starts to speak, what sort of results can you deduce by his way of talking, choice of words, and voice intonation? Can you predict what will be his next action before he actually does it? Can you read his thoughts and foretell what will be his next words before he actually speaks them? Interestingly, if he is observant enough, he may be doing the same as you are doing without letting you realize him analyzing you.

This subtle perception and personality analysis are actually an inevitable part of our life. Even if a person is quite untrained in the art of human behavioral classification and mind-reading, he still consciously or unconsciously pays attention to certain things. Without even realizing this, he automatically notices his cohabiters, his friends, his surroundings, his subordinates, and his own reactions to their stimulating actions or their reactions to his own actions. The people are all a part of a beaded chain interlinked together. A nudge in a particular direction will cause a bead to move and nudge the adjacent one until all of them are moving and passing through the thread. If one of them is stuck in the way, it will become a hurdle in harmonious flow and movement. Similarly, the ripple effect in the waterworks.

Most of us have experience in playing stone skipping. Upon throwing the flat stone into the water bed, mostly, your eyes are focused on the stone to follow the number of bounces. However, the alternative way to look at this or the other side of the picture will be to focus on the water that has been subjected to the ripple effect. How interestingly, one circular wave pattern nudges the other, and that other one touches another until an influential pattern is formed that starts inwardly and expands outwardly. This effect is a clear message to us analyzers that just like the stone causing multiple ripples in the water, an action or behavior of a person can also be continuously influential and crucial in several given situations.

You must have heard countless times the saying: Think before you act. But the truth there is far more to this statement that just thinking and doing. Aligning your intention with your action is just not enough. Instead, you must align your intention with the possible outcome of your action. Here you think what actually does it mean? Confused? Don't be! It simply means to predict how a person you are addressing your words to will possibly behave in response to those words and how your intended actions can affect him. This can be mastered by understanding human personality analysis.

The human mind, as a subject of study, makes an interesting book for reading if one is a bibliophile. However, even if you aren't an avid reader, it can still prove to be an exhilarating ride to experience. In this book, you can imagine a book within a book! We shall be discussing some of those concepts that serve as chapters of the book of the human mind along with the consequent benefits of speed-reading people, psychological intricacies of the organ called mind, and the relationship between mind, body, and actions.

CHAPTER 2

BENEFITS OF ANALYZING PEOPLE AND BASICS OF HUMAN BEHAVIORAL PSYCHOLOGY

Personality is a fascinating concept in human behavioral psychology. While behavior defines the actions and manners of a person, personality itself is a collection of those behaviors. You can say that behavior is a building block of personality. The human personality is a unique set of characteristic traits, thinking patterns, and actions. Each individual has a specific set of behaviors that distinguishes him from his counterparts. The behavioral psychologists and personality development experts have classified several types of human personality according to individual differences and unique trait patterns that emerge together as a unified whole forming a persona.

According to research, paradigms are behaviors set of conceptual thoughts that help us identify a person's habits and the motivation behind his actions. Then this paradigm can sometimes experience either a sudden or a more gradual shift that reconditions the entire thought process of an individual. A question might arise that why should we, while analyzing people, try to see their point of view? The answer to this question leads to our changed attitude towards public dealing. Each individual possessing individual thoughts, is, in fact, also a participant of a global thought process.

Psychology is a science that may seem quite clichéd to most people but is actually a very layered scientific domain. It deals with various real yet abstract concepts that may seem complex at the surface, but once studied in a systematic manner, it can lead to more concrete approaches. Behavioral psychology is also a part of a much wider domain, and itself has many subdomains. It is closely linked to cognitive psychology and deals with concepts such as behavior, learning, stimulus, response, reinforcements, habit formation, environment, mental schemas, conditioning, and cognitive reprogramming.

If a person aims to be successful in life, his ambition alone will not be enough. Numerous hindrances may occur in his path to the successful accomplishment of the desired goals and objectives in life. This is because we don't live in a crystal ball isolated from others. We are a social animal. Socialization is our breathing lifeline. We cannot expect the life's path to be linear and one dimensional in a way that nothing crosses us while traveling that path. The fact is that each person's pathway in life intersects or connects at some point with other pathways. At that point, one needs to be well prepared for facing the world and its people. It is vitally important to be able to analyze how people think, act, and react and to be able to understand what they intend, plan, and expect. This benefits us in achieving not only our own objectives but also clearing the path for someone else too. It may be termed as some sort of symbiotic relationship in humans.

The key to success is an appropriate paradigm shift, and the key to shifting your paradigm or someone else's is to understand people in general. Public smartness is key to a successful approach towards goal setting and action planning. It is also instrumental in effective communication and socialization.

Think hard, why would people want to be remembered by someone, and why would you want to remember them? It is mainly because of the fact that a particularly striking trait of their behavior catches your eye and remains in your mind for quite a long time.

People tend to stereotype others by typecasting them into fixed categories. However, to see a person standing out in a crowd, we must seem to understand that particular, striking quality of an individual that sets him apart from others. Your old friends from school will be forever remembered by you, even if you have made dozens of newer friends in both college and professional life. Not just because they were dearer to you, but also because you spent more time with them, paid more attention to them, and each one of the group was known for some of their striking, unique traits. Maybe it was a nosy attitude of Anna, or a lazy persona of Tyler, or an untidy appearance of Sam, or loud laughter of Ben. All of these were memorable traits that distinguished them, so they remained in your mind for a long time.

Now, coming towards your newer friends, you may also be able to understand and remember them if you were truly interested, but the point here is not just to remember for the sake of memory. The point is, to be able to understand them in order to shape your own attitude towards them in a constructive manner until they respond to you in the same manner. This is also called behavioral conditioning or public programming.

This concept also becomes greatly beneficial in the business and professional arena. Recruitment, retention, and appraisals, etc. are all a part of a professional employment routine. There is a whole branch of business administration dedicated to people management called Human Resource management. The HR department deals with the tasks mentioned above and much more regularly, and job analysis is a big part of it. The job analysis not only helps organizations in the determination of suitable employee choices for a particular role, but it also helps them study in detail the potential candidates' behavior, abilities, mindset, and expected work outcomes. The interviews are also a major tool in determining the most suitable candidate among the applicants by analyzing them and understanding their work objectives, ambitions, perception, and ethics.

The human personality analysis has become so influential in taking major decisions in various aspects of life that experts nowadays are emphasizing more on the importance of soft, life skills and emotional intelligence than on academic achievements and high grades. This may be because now, people are gaining awareness on how living successfully and surviving in practical scenarios is more important than just attending schools to gain formal, idealistic education. Confronting the practicality of life needs one to remove the rose-tinted glasses from the eyes. To see the world experientially, one must realize the interdependence of its dwellers on each other. Though, this was not the case centuries back. In primitive ages, the humans were quite caught up in their own isolated living area. There were seldom any interactions or communication. No particular language was operational. The basics such as eating, sleeping, hunting, and protecting, etc. were the main daily activities in order to survive. We can say that humans were indeed just starting to climb Maslow's Pyramid of human needs or the Hierarchy of Human Motivation. The first step in the pyramid is the need for fulfillment of the basic physiological necessities such as air, shelter, food, clothing, sleep, etc. That is what primitive man did and require.

However, now that the times have evolved, humans have become more civilized and intellectualized. They have learned to make protective shelters, modern buildings, and health maintenance centers for themselves. They have learned to lighten the darkness and darken the light with just a click of a switch. They have learned to speak several languages in order to communicate for the sake of cohabitation, trading, teaching, learning, writing, and simply understanding each other. They have continued to climb higher in the hierarchy, and there are certain motivations that seem to be the driving force in pursuing the fulfillment of each stage of the needs.

Whether it be physical or physiological, security or safety, love and belonging, esteem, or self-actualization, each stage comprises a set of human needs that are driven by certain motivations in order to be fulfilled.

CHAPTER 3

OBSERVATION, RECOGNITION, AND EVALUATION

A nalyzing the people proves to be quite enjoyable and informative if followed in an organized pattern. The process has a path paved with some proposed milestones. Reaching them can ensure the successful journey of learning people's behavior and reading their minds. Embarking on this journey, the three components of the initial milestone are observation, recognition, and evaluation.

Observation:

Imagine yourself as a microscope, the world being your subject of study. How many wondrous revelations can you unveil by just observing carefully and closely? Experts view that every human upon birth is bestowed with a special kind of mental power to observe and explore the surroundings. A baby's mind has this innate ability to take in impressions from the environment and absorb them. This observational absorption of information occurs initially at an unconscious stage but soon transforms into a conscious effort on an individual's part. This way, not only mental muscles are created, but also the observational mentality becomes operational.

At an early age, the mind is so special that the acquisition of knowledge occurs naturally. Listening to sounds, touching surfaces, smelling fragrances, etc. These small sensory actions can make an individual literate in the workings of the world he lives in. However, afterward, the concentration and conscious effort begin to play a vital role in making this knowledge more comprehensible and more profoundly meaningful. Observation, at its best, can be an instrument for gaining insightful knowledge. Using that knowledge, one can derive conclusions that facilitate growth and development in a holistic manner.

Recognition:

As time passes, a person becomes more informed and knowledgeable about his environment. He begins to recognize things and identify them. This stage of recognition is quite influential. It can make or break a concept and shift the mental paradigm completely. However, this recognition concept is closely dependent on existing mental schemas and preset wiring of the brain. A person recognizes an old thing as he has perceived it before. Or he recognizes a new thing mostly based on his perception of similar looking things.

A kid, upon seeing a cat, is told that it is called a cat and it has four legs. Now, upon seeing another animal with four legs that he has never seen before, he is likely to call it a cat, too. This is because the first time he saw a cat, his mind took an impression and saved it. A mental structure was formed, adding or storing this knowledge in the brain. The second time a stimulating image of a similar-looking animal was shown to him, the mind combed through previous knowledge to come up with possible explanation or name for the new image. Thus what the brain stores in there, is what the brain represents again and again unless a new schema is formed or an older one gets adjusted to the newer information. This is what we call mental reprogramming. So, when the observer is taking notice of his surrounding environment or meets people, he is likely to form opinions and recognize different signs and behaviors. This recognition would be according to his mental conditioning unless he learns techniques to analyze people in a systematic manner.

Evaluation:

The third stage is Evaluation. As the name suggests, to evaluate means to asses, analyze, and form an idea about a thing or concept. The word "analyze" cannot be interchangeably used with evaluating because both of them have some distinguishing features that define them. Analysis means to break a whole into parts and study these parts to understand the whole. Evaluation means to determine or estimate the significance of a concept. Mostly, after the observation and recognition of a concept or behavior, the observer analyzes it by interpreting each part carefully and then evaluate it by realizing and determining the impact and significance of each part of the observed behavior or incident. The evaluation helps in deriving the results and reaching to possible conclusions and explanations. It can also give way to post-observational reflections and realizations. By following the implications suggested by an effective evaluation, an observer is led to an improved personality change and behavioral positivity. In theory, evaluation should be an unbiased judgment. However, experts recommend the observation should be unbiased, based on factually objective data while evaluation can be a personal assessment of that data.

Week 1

Let us start our first week of understanding the basics of analyzing people by learning the first three techniques, as mentioned below.

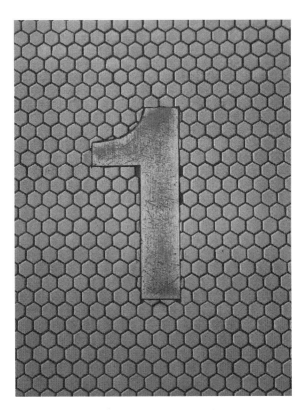

TECHNIQUE 1: OBSERVING THE SURROUNDINGS

Experts in behavioral psychology say that one of the most troublesome hindrances faced by mankind in leading a successful life today is an appropriate reaction to corresponding stimuli. The surroundings you live in may seem quite familiar to you in a way that you tend to lose interest in observing them. Eventually, it becomes a habit, and even if you go somewhere else, to an unfamiliar place, your lack of observational curiosity catches up to you there as well. However, you must understand that you have to build this habit in you to observe places, people, objects, vehicles, etc. anything that constitutes the environment surrounding you or the person you intend to analyze. The first technique is to just perceive and observe. Looking is to notice something; seeing or perceiving is to notice it intelligently; observing is to not only noticing it but taking notes as well, i.e., recording it or retaining it in mind carefully.

While performing observation, the observer must be patient and persevering. Accurateness and attention is the key to gather productive information. Be careful about noticing the details in order to avoid missing even a single nuance. Sometimes, a little bit of change in one's behavior can be a root cause of action, and people not keen on their observations often tend to miss or overlook that exact particular change. Try to avoid being that careless observer if you want to be successful in your analysis.

The following action steps will summarize this technique more comprehensively:

Select a subject of study, i.e., a person whom you intend to analyze.

Keep in mind the goal of your observation. An aimless observation mostly serves as a distraction and a cognitive traffic jammer, instead of being a purposeful activity.

Concentrate, as it is the key to gathering sufficient information through observation. When you are concentrating on the person, you zero your sensory powers on him, indicating to the brain how important this analysis is to you. Therefore, the brain exercises its full potential in noticing things about the subject.

Keep in mind the preliminary data or background information, if possible. However, an observation from scratch can also be useful in the case of practical strangers.

Pursue your task at hand with singular obsession, i.e., don't multi-task at this time. Just be calm and pay attention. Calmness helps in increasing the focus and saves the energy as a back up to be used.

Be as objective as you can in order to form an independent perspective.

Make sure the observation is as subtle as possible. You don't want to be labeled as a stalker or staring freak. Remember, you are the one who is noticing, not the one being noticed.

Consider all the possible sources of information while performing the observation.

Keep in mind that, although, the methods may be quite similar to scientific observation, observing people can be a bit prejudicial even if only in an unconscious way. This can be avoided by consciously clearing your mind from previous stereotypes and biases.

TECHNIQUE 2: RECOGNIZING THE ENVIRONMENTAL FACTORS

The second technique is recognizing environmental factors. The surrounding environment of a person you mean to analyze is actually a maze that hides several unearthed traits. Once you begin to observe closely, you feel a certain curiosity to explore and recognize things in a meaningful manner in order to understand each thing's purpose and functionality. Also, this recognition will help you understand how a certain person behaves and why he does so. The environment has a close relationship with the psychology of the human mind. Environmental psychology is a whole branch of psychological sciences dedicated to the relationship between living organisms and their surrounding environment. As mentioned previously, a human being is not an isolated creature manufactured as a standalone book. It is just one book in a huge chain of books. Then these books are arranged on different shelves located in different book stores. To determine the exact location and situational setting of a particular piece, you have to closely observe and explore the surroundings.

Mainly any environment has two types of factors that influence the people living there. These factors are either external or internal in nature. Both of these factors are instrumental in impacting an individual and his surrounding environment. External environmental factors include economic, social, educational, climatic, geographic, technical, media, etc. These are also called outer influencers. Whereas, the internal environmental factors or influencers include moral values, cultural norms, and traditions, motivations, attitudes, and beliefs, etc.

A person is greatly influenced by these factors. A deep look into the culture of a community or society will let us know about the common beliefs, habits, and expected behaviors of the people residing there. Further observation and recognition of the influence of media sources such as newspapers, journals, books, internet websites and portals, radio and television channels, will let us know changes that may have occurred in the demographics of a particular region. The mindset change occurs when these factors are present in the environment. The trick is to keep these in mind while analyzing a person. Also, the constant practice can help you recognize these elemental influencers that work in the background more quickly.

Recognize how the social setting is shaped and how the person you are analyzing gels or fits in.

Recognize the climate and geographic setting of the place.

Recognize the educational, economic, and emotional background of the person.

Recognize the influence of technology, print, and social media on the dwellers in an area.

Recognize the school of thought or belief to which a person you are analyzing belongs.

Recognize the cultural differences and moral values that might affect a person's outlook.

Remember that all the recognized factors can be crucial to your analysis in one way or the other. Don't underestimate the importance of any one of them.

Review once again and make sure that the subject person indeed seems to belong to that particular environment of which you have recognized the factors.

The above action steps will be fruitful in making use of the observational efforts you made following the first technique and will help in progressing with the third technique.

TECHNIQUE 3: EVALUATING THE TRAITS AND OTHER IMPACTS

This technique involves the detailed assessment of environmental factors that you have recognized before. As the process of evaluation ensures that the gathered information is categorized systematically and understood for its impactful significance, the determination of the impact of each one of the environmental influencers on an individual is important. This can be ensured by first examining each recognized factor in detail. Understanding its range, capacity, and power of influence is vital to determine its significance.

For example, after observing a person's surroundings and environmental situation carefully, you recognized an externally influential factor, i.e., education. Now, the action step is to delve deeper into the impact of this factor on that particular person. Determine how it might be affecting his behavior, speech, and action. How and what capacity of behavioral change and personality improvement is possible due to this factor, i.e., acquiring education. To what extent or range has he actually been successful in gaining the education and how much time he has spent in doing so. These assessed facts can change your perspective about a person, and this can help you in understanding them better because you become more aware of their intellectual speech, or from where they are coming from while seeming to be pretentious at first glance.

Consider another, more practical example; while you are observing a person, you recognize that he is quite averse to eating with a spoon or fork, etc. You recognize that he belongs to a particular culture where eating with the hand is preferred. While evaluating these facts and their impact, you may reach to a more positive conclusion that the significantly different culture has prompted this behavior consciously or unconsciously rather than lack of table manners. Therefore, it becomes apparent that people should be analyzed, keeping these factors in mind. If these techniques are practiced at the initial phase of your journey, you will be better capable to aptly take notice of individual differences that are vital in shaping the person's thoughts and behaviors.

To summarize the action steps for the technique of evaluation, consider these points:

✓ After recognition of both the external and internal influencers, make sure to delimitate the subject's surroundings so that your mind doesn't wander around unmarked territories.

✓ Refresh the recognized information in mind.

✓ Reflect on the gathered information. Reflection is the essence of observation. There can be no possibility of improvement and development, nor can there be solutions or conclusions without practicing the art of reflection. The reflection explores questions like what happened, how it happened, why did it happen or what does it mean, and what might this implicate for the future?

✓ Analyze the factors by decoding the collective information into chunks and assessing each one's relationship with the person separately.

✓ Design sub-questions. Reflection can be more systematic if followed by properly designing the underlying questions to ask and enquire such as how could social media have impacted the person in question, or why does a person prefer to sit down on the floor instead of on the chair? or what level of economic/financial difficulty might have forced this highly experienced person to seek entry-level employment? There can be a long list of possible scenarios and questions that may be developed to analyze and evaluate a person's behavior.

✓ Create a strategic process for seeking answers to these questions such as meeting, communicating, and discussing.

✓ Derive results and conclude the information.

✓ Compliment your evaluated information by personal statements or perspective.

CHAPTER 4

BEHAVIOR, MOTIVATION, AND PERSONALITY

In previous chapters, the definition of behavior and personality was mentioned. In this chapter, we will discuss the relationship of these with another important component of human psychology, i.e., motivation. Motivation defines the reason or cause of the action of an individual. It also happens to be the driving force behind each goal a person sets, or each struggle he undergoes to achieve the desired object. Without the motivational push, an individual's behaviors are in a state of chaos, so the personality also becomes confused and disoriented. The root word of motivation is motive meaning a certain need to accomplish something.

Psychology experts say that humans are controlled by their own minds unless they learn to control it themselves. The needs, desires, and wishes are the one that guides our actions. We become a slave to them if we follow them blindly and obligingly. The personality becomes controlled and submissive to these compulsive urges. To understand this, consider an example of a street boy who has no money to pay for the cheeseburger he so craves. There is a nearby stall where a vendor is selling hot, yummy cheeseburgers. The boy is passing by the stall, in his ragged appearance. Initially, he attempts to come and beg for his desirous food, but the vendor tells him off in a sneering manner. Now, if he becomes a slave to his hunger, he might submit to the need to steal or deceive.

Analyzing his behavior, we may not subject his whole personality to be of a thief, but we may name this particular behavior like stealing, on a superficial inspection at least. However, still, we cannot say that his motive was to steal. Instead, for him, this served as a means to an end. We are not here to justify his actions, of course, but a possible explanation can be given to explore his underlying motivation to do what he did. Remember, analysis is to understand the behavior rather than justify it, though an explanation and looking deeper into other's perspectives unveils contrary beliefs and personality traits that defy one's apparent actions or behaviors.

Some behavioral psychologists may explain motivation as an impulsive thought or notion. Montessori theory suggests that home is always present in the sub-conscience of the human mind. A person's will to perform an action sometimes gets intercepted by hormetic impulses. A sudden motivation to exhibit a particular behavior can expose the inner desires of an individual's mind. Most people are quite secretive and expressionless. By predicting the possible motivation behind their actions, one can follow their behavioral pattern. This can help in locating the behaviors that may occur, reoccur, or never occur according to the situational need. In a given circumstance, if your subject did a certain action or reacted in a certain way, what sort of need possessed him to do it? What could be his motive? What is the possibility that he may react in a similar manner if he finds himself in the same situation again, plus or minus, any factor? These questions can be answered if closer attention is paid to the relationship between the behavior, motivation, and personality of an individual.

Week 2:

So, dear reader, have you reviewed and practiced the techniques mentioned throughout the previous week? If yes, it is time for proceeding to the next week's techniques. If no, now is your chance to go back a few pages and refresh what you read previously. So without further ado, let us start our second week with some fresh techniques.

TECHNIQUE 4: RECORDING THE BEHAVIOR PATTERN

After understanding the basics of the relationship between the behavior, personality, and motivation, the main step is to record the pattern in which behavior is occurring. As we have briefly mentioned an example of behavior and personality traits previously, we will focus more on the active aspect of behavior patterns here both in theory and practice.

The research experts in the field of psychological behaviorism suggest several special patterns to classify certain behaviors. Some argue that behavioral psychology is quite different from cognitive psychology in the sense that the former is based on the theory of behavior change with respect to the experiences of an individual. While the latter suggests that the behaviors are cognitive reactions to sensory impulses and can be processed and reprocessed according to the cognitive functionality, willpower, and determination of the human mind. The behaviorists emphasize that the behavior pattern is entirely dependent on the external stimulus while cognitive psychologists argue that the behavior pattern can be defined by the way knowledge is encoded, stored, and processed in our cognition. However, to make it simple and applicable, both theories are two different angles of the same picture, i.e., a behavior pattern forms when an individual responds to an external stimulus using his internal senses gains experience, learns things, stores them in his mind, and reiterates his action in a similar, recurring situation.

When we go for a shopping trip, we observe many different shops in the market. Among them are dress shops, jewelry shops, book shops, shoe shops, pharmacies, nurseries, bakeries, grocery shops, etc. If you enter one of them, you are directed to aisles of organized items displayed with proper classification of each category they belong to. For instance, dresses are arranged according to their color, size, structure, and price. If you choose a particular dress, you do so according to your taste. Your taste is defined by your personality. Just like that, your behaviors shaping your personality are also classified and defined by your motivational instinct that, due to recurrence, evolves into a habitual pattern.

- If you wear white, formal dresses on Fridays at work, your particular clothing style becomes your habit displaying a recurring behavior.

- If a student is late in the class for the first time, it may look like an exceptional scenario. However, if he is late every day, he forms a pattern of tardiness which is a type of behavior.

- If a writer researches a topic for the first time, then writes the content, he would not be called a vigorous researcher. Research is a type of behavior. A series of similar research actions performed in succession in order to create each informative piece of content in a consistent manner may exhibit a behavioral pattern and thus, a writer can be called a researcher, too.

Observational psychologists use multiple tools to record behavioral patterns. These tools may include event sampling, time sampling, rubrics, checklists, running records, anecdotal records, portfolios, performance charts, action memos, etc. Some people interested in analyzing the behavior sets often use customized graphs and legends to records the reactions and responses of a person being observed. Audio recordings, pictures, and other media tools may also help in this regard.

TECHNIQUE 5: DECODING THE MOTIVATION (INTRINSIC + EXTRINSIC)

This technique involves the action step of decoding and evaluating the motivational factors working behind the scenes. Each one of them plays a vital role in dictating a particular set of actions. The term extrinsic refers to the external motivational factors, while the term intrinsic is dedicated to the internal factors of motivation.

The concept of rewards and punishment seems to be closely related to the motivational factors governing an individual's personality. The well-known theory of behavioral psychology called operant conditioning is based on the philosophy of reinforcements or consequences.

A reinforcement is basically a motivational reward to reinforce or strengthen the desired behavior so that it is repeatedly occurring in a consistent manner. It can be either positive or negative. In positive reinforcement, some desired stimulus or motivational factor is added to generate an intended behavior. Whereas, in negative reinforcement, some undesired stimulus or demotivating factor is taken away or removed in order to generate intended behavior.

✓ For instance, examine how an employee is conditioned to perform well in the presence of a dangling motivation of getting a promotion or a salary raise. Here, good work performance is the intended behavior and the rise in salary or offer of a promotion is the positive reinforcement (something that is going to be given instead of being taken away, to ensure the repetition of similar behavior).

✓ Now, consider a similar scenario in the context of negative reinforcement. An employee is working in an organization that has set some rewards for good work performance. If a person performs well and his work meets the quality standards in a consistent manner, some of his weekly quota of tasks will be lessened to take away the burden. Here, the intended behavior is the same, i.e., good work performance, but right now, it is strengthened or reinforced by removing or taking away an undesired factor, i.e., workload from the person.

Similarly, behavior patterns can also be analyzed by the consequences or the punishing factors that serve as demotivators. If a particular behavior is weakened and not occurring again, it may be because there is some fear of punishment or consequence. Learners are often trained to obey by this sort of operant conditioning. The consequences, too, can be both negative or positive. The rule is the same. If a particularly undesired behavior is recurring in an individual, and its pattern should be weakened, a punishment acts as a stimulus. If an undesired object is added or given to the individual as a punishment to inhibit the bad behavior, it is called positive punishment. If, however, a desired outcome or object is removed or taken away from an individual in an attempt to punish or weaken his resolve so that the bad behavior does not occur again, it is called negative punishment.

✓ For instance, you are analyzing a student, and you have recorded his behavior pattern. Whenever there is a possibility of extra lessons as a punishment for making noise in the class, he becomes obediently silent. This is actually positive punishment because here, an undesired stimulus, i.e., extra lessons, is added to weaken or inhibit an unrequired or bad behavioral pattern (making noise).

✓ Similarly, the same student is motivated to inhibit his undesirable behavior by taking away his desired activity or stimulus, i.e., play period or recess time. In this case, the punishment would be called as negative punishment.

The possibility of these consequences or rewards may motivate or stimulate a person to act or react in a particular behavioral pattern. To exhibit a good or generally desired behavior, an individual can be motivated by extrinsic factors such as:

- Monetary incentives
- Promotional offers
- Encouragement
- Complimentary rewards
- Honors and Certificates
- Appreciation statements

- Performance grading

- Appraisals and applause

- Claps and Badges

- Material gifts

- Greeting cards

- Consolation prizes

- Trophies and medals

- Fame and popularity

- Good reputation, etc.

Whereas, the intrinsic motivational factors are generally related to internal, intangible feelings, emotions, thoughts, and objectives that are governed by your own mind. They may have some interdependency on the extrinsic factors but are mostly personal in nature. The internal drive or urge to succeed, prove yourself, or internal fears can be counted as intrinsic impulses. The positive and negative intrinsic factors of motivation are basically reciprocal of each other. For instance, a person may be motivated by his determination to complete the work on time, or he may be motivated by his lack of determination, to procrastinate. The major intrinsic motivational factors are listed below. Imagine the opposite of each one of them in a contrasting scenario.

- Internal satisfaction
- Enjoyment
- Intention
- Wishes and desires
- Curiosity
- Purpose
- Passion
- Self-confidence (or lack of it)
- Determination (or lack of it)
- Personality growth
- Knowledge acquisition
- Autonomy and freedom
- Love or a sense of belonging
- Compassion
- Security and shelter
- Hunger
- Dedication
- Commitment
- Promise
- Guilt

- Self-consciousness

- Distress

- Sleepiness

- Hesitation

- Complexes such as inferiority or superiority complex, etc.

After decoding the particular motivation factors that are involved in the exhibition of a specific behavioral pattern, you can be able to understand the triggering elements that govern the personality of an individual. You can apply this technique on various subjects, practicing throughout the week, and progressing on your journey about analyzing people.

TECHNIQUE 6: UNDERSTANDING THE PERSONALITY MODEL

This technique is the final one in this week's action steps. The time for understanding the personality model has come. Till now, we were practicing the single bits and pieces of the personality that is the behavior and its patterns. However, after a thorough understanding of behaviors and how the motivations behind each of them can impact an individual, the personality, as a whole, is to be understood.

First, let us know some more about the background of the personality models theory. In the past, there were many theories about personality traits and classifying them into models of identifiable behavior was a subject of constant study by psychologists. The more researches emerged, the more transition occurred in the explanation of personality models. The verbal factor analysis became quite a tool to classify and define specific personality traits and categorize them as regular models. Several studies were conducted until recent years when finally, this theory became more simplified and applicable. Even though there are some other personality models prevalent, this one has a more verbal and simpler approach, so we will be discussing this particular model under technique number 6. Known as the Big-Five-Traits personality set or Five-Factor Model (FFM), this set of carefully picked traits comprises of 5 different broad personality aspects. They are named as OCEAN:

- O for Openness
- C for Conscientiousness
- E for Extraversion
- A for Agreeableness
- N for Neuroticism

Each of these trait names is actually named after the verbal descriptors for five vast domains or dimensions of human behavior and psyche. These traits have two sub-aspects each, depicting two extremes in a person's behavior.

These extremes can be stated as:

- Openness (to experience) = Curious or Inventive v/s

Cautious or Consistent

- Conscientiousness = Organized or Efficient v/s Careless or Easy-going

- Extraversion = Energetic or Outgoing v/s Reserved or Solitary

- Agreeableness = Compassionate or Friendly v/s Detached or Challenging

- Neuroticism = Confident or Secure v/s Nervous or Sensitive

This model is based on the verbal descriptor analysis method in which a selected set of descriptive words having related meanings can be used to describe a personality verbally, yet still managing to paint a visual picture of the behavioral patterns exhibited by it.

✓ In the above categories, the word openness (to experience) describes the willingness to learn experientially, explore new things, and create or generate new concepts and ideas. It explains an open, welcoming attitude that portrays a broadminded, revolutionary outlook of a person in his life.

For instance, an individual who is open to experience may possess traits like curiosity, industriousness, inventiveness, revolution, progressiveness, pragmatism, innovation, mobility, radicalism, creativity, spontaneity, and inquisitiveness. Similarly, the person who is not open to experience may possess traits like cautiousness, conservativeness, wariness to unfamiliar concepts, consistency, regularity, predictability, repetitiveness, stagnation, uniformity, etc. You can identify similar word patterns and descriptors in each category mentioned above and understand how the two extremes work in contrast, shaping the two sorts of personality models among the people.

✓ The word conscientiousness means to be organized, diligent, efficient, meticulous, careful, guarded, detailed, attentive, dedicated, punctual, principled, thorough, etc. The lack of this would portray a personality possessing traits such as carelessness, inefficiency, chaos, lazy, lax, unprincipled, easy-going, superficial, unscrupulous, etc. The word conscientiousness is actually an indicator that an individual falling under this category and scoring high on the positive extreme of the domain would have high regard for conscious actions and morality. A strong sense of right and wrong can be present in the person that acts according to his conscience. On the contrary, the person scoring negative on this domain's chart, graph, or the list would tend to exhibit immorality and unprincipled attitude.

✓ The word extraversion technically means to be an extrovert, i.e., easily sociable and interactive. The traits such as talkativeness, sociability, assertiveness, interactivity, gregariousness, outgoingness, friendliness, demonstrativeness, affability, companionability, unreservedness, etc. The lack of extraversion would lead to another extreme involving traits such as shyness, introversion, reservedness, reticence, hesitance, nervousness, isolation, withdrawal, unsociability, self-consciousness, self-efficacy, self-reliance, disinterest, etc.

✓ The term agreeableness is meant to describe

characteristics such as tactfulness, warmth, assertiveness, positivity, calmness, attachment, compassion, amiability, nicety, lovability, consideration, kindness, sympathy, and cooperativeness. The opposite of these traits would be harshness, unfeelingness, detachment, indifference, aloofness, remoteness, offensiveness, disagreeableness, uncaringness, repulsiveness, displeasure, negativity, obnoxiousness, etc.

✓ The word Neuroticism is actually derived from the neuroscientific term called neurosis, which means mental impairment or illness that is relatively mild in nature. The derived word neuroticism describes the category of the personality model in the presence of which, people exhibit traits such as nervousness, stress, discomfort, hesitation, turmoil, oversensitiveness, anxiety, anger, jealousy, possessiveness, frustration, fear, guilt, depression, worriedness, moodiness, etc. On the other hand, the lack of neuroticism or a negative range or ranking on the scale of neuroticism may exhibit contrasting traits such as confidence, sense of security and independence, self-content, composure, mental stability, control, collectedness, relaxedness, tranquility, serenity, ease, poise, coolness, etc.

Pioneers of this personality model state that these five domains are so vast and all-inclusive that they encompass all the people out there. Every individual falls under at least one of these categories. Study carefully and understand the person who is to be the subject of your analysis. In which category or under how many categories he may fall and what sort of combinations can be made out of his personality traits after a thorough analysis. Which extremes are apparent in his personality?

CHAPTER 5

WHAT IS MIND READING?

I s mind reading possible? Can humans actually read the emotions and thoughts of a person? Mind reading sounds like a superpower coming straight out of comics. While you cannot communicate with someone miles away from you like Charles Xavier, you can certainly learn this useful skill by gaining knowledge, constant practice, focus, and a certain level of experience. In this chapter, we will discuss some tricks you can learn and apply to read other people's minds. There's something you need to know about mind-reading before you scroll down to learn about these practical tips for getting into someone's head.

Mind Reading - Humans' Inbuilt Feature

Humans are programmed and designed in such a way that it is our second nature to read other people's minds as we interact with them. You might not realize this, but it might have been practiced by you from time to time in your everyday life. The moment you spelled out something and your friend had said at that exact instant, "How do you know I was going to say that?" Just there, you read that person's mind, anticipating the word(s) and uttering it before your friend could say it. This inbuilt ability is present there, and it just needs to be practiced more and more so that it can be polished. Anyone determined enough to polish and sharpen this ability of his cognitive domain should take note of the fact that every human around him has been emitting some sort of an aura or vibes. This may seem such a metaphysical concept, but it is quite true. Your negative or positive feelings may get rub off on someone or vice versa. You can learn to read minds by paying attention to these details. It's just about regaining focus and practicing the following tips:

1. Don't Ignore the Generation Gap

Boomers and Millennials have different values and thinking process. You can learn so much about how a person thinks just by knowing which generation they belong to. Millennials are usually not very social as compared to Boomers. Many Millennials also enjoy jobs which makes them feel independent such as home-based jobs. Boomers, on the other hand, prefer to be on the field and also are more open to face-to-face conversations.

2. Examine Body Language

Body language plays a huge role in reading minds, as will be discussed in upcoming chapters in more detail. Here just note this down as an action step.

Isolate the person from the surroundings imaginatively and focus just on the body of the person. When having a conversation, observe if the person is attentive, does the person looks down, change face direction, or move backward. These are signs that the person is not engaged with you. If someone leans towards you when you speak, it may be interpreted that he is paying attention to what you're saying.

3. Listen Attentively

In a conversation, listen carefully. Having good listening skills can reveal a ton of information about someone's thoughts and emotions. Observe the tone when someone speaks, enthusiasm and frustration are easily recognized. Your welcoming attitude should also encourage others to talk with you as much as possible. The more someone talks, the more they will reveal about themselves.

4. Start a Conservation

A conversation can be a key to someone's thoughts. Asking the right questions is crucial. What does the person value? On what topic you would likely get a strong response? Tell them stories and issues from your own life; more likely than not; they will agree that they have the same or similar issues. This way, you will get a deeper understanding of there problems and their mental state.

5. Personality as a Determinant

As discussed previously, human beings have vastly different personalities. Learning about personalities will make you determine someone's characteristics and what they find significant. An introvert will avoid gatherings and would like to spend time alone rather than hanging out with a group, while an extrovert will prefer to spend time socializing freely.

Mind Reading, Some More Insight:

Mind reading is the art of gaining absolute power within the cognitive realm of someone. It is not some sort of supernatural magic. Instead, cognitive psychology experts call it a scientific technique involving major cognitive functions such as perception, reasoning, concentration, memorization, and comprehension. It works on the principle of neuroelectric activity taking place in the brain. The electric impulses or neurochemical messages are actually bioelectric signals that make our thoughts, memories, emotions, and feelings a collection of tangible mental structures that are wired systematically in a certain order or manner. The brain works each activity at a different frequency. The subconscious has a relatively lower current or frequency level than the conscious state of mind.

The mind control experts even use a motor car example to describe the microcontroller, i.e., special-purpose computer, characteristics of the brain. At high voltage, the mind generates numerous neuro transmitting impulses that makes the thinking process faster. The mind-reading can also be possible through tangible electronic machines depicting frequencies and impulse wavelengths. The police investigation methods and special screening tests have been invented to use these techniques for reading a person's mind to detect lies, treachery, fear, inhibitions, excitement, and several other emotions and thoughts. What happens is that these detectors or wave readers are attached to a person, scanning his brain, and they can notify when a particular synaptic pathway becomes operational due to the transmission of the neurochemical messages. Numerous researches are still underway to develop this field further.

How to Speed-Read People?

The curiously amazing fact of life is the powerhouse of your entire functioning and actions remain invisible to you. The human mind and the thoughts running in it make up your entire psyche yet; they are often veiled behind the confines of the brain box. The mind-power is interdependent with the other physical forces like experiences, objects, people, etc. The power of a mind to create, think, and analyze wonderfully abundant yet very rarely gets to be used to its full potential.

Speed-reading people is a technique that aims at analyzing people in a quick, definite way according to some pre-decided cues and clues. This is a source of interpretation of both the personality traits and thinking patterns of a person you are analyzing. In the past, reading was limited to books and journals; now, the times have changed. To gain knowledge, traditional reading and studying are not enough. You have to take notice of physical surroundings, observe people, understand their emotions and actions, and learn from life experiences.

The method of speed-reading initially was used to push the brain to deliver its maximum output. The boost to the cognition often results in optimum performance. The person reading an average of 200-250 words per minute is often pushed to perform fast and improve his reading by 600 wpm almost. This is made possible by applying several cues and techniques to the reading method used in order to bring improvement. Now, in the same way, a person observing another individual may overlook many cues if he is a slow or uninterested reader or lacks the necessary skills. If he wants to perform a quick analysis, he must speed up the things.

The speed is gained when you accumulate these skills while reading people:

✓ **Interest:** You must be interested in your subject, i.e., the person you aim to read.

✓ **Attentiveness:** You must pay attention to minutest details and not miss or overlook anything.

✓ **Confidence:** You must be confident in your

observational skills. You must not shy away from glancing around, or look straight into the eyes of the subject in order to read signs, movements, or specific expressions.

✓ **Objectivity:** You must look at the person without prejudice or personal bias in order to gain impartial insight into his personality.

✓ **Concentration:** You must solely be concentrating on the person you are analyzing. Your mind should act as a converging lens, focusing all thoughts on reading that person.

✓ **Clarity of objective:** You must know beforehand why you are speed-reading the person and why you have selected him for this purpose. Make your intentions and goals clear in your mind to speed up the process as confusion slows down the things.

✓ **Dedication:** You must be willing to spend your time speed-reading people. If you cannot dedicate a few minutes of your time observing your subject, do not expect to understand him quickly.

✓ ***Order:*** You must put your thoughts and acquired insights into an organized pattern to draw sensible, reasonable conclusions. It will be easier to start the reading in a logical sequence such as body language, nonverbal clues, then verbal communication cues, etc.

After making sure these skills are aligned in your goal setting, you can begin to practice speed-reading people with ease and familiarity. The following techniques will let you know the action steps of this process in detail.

TECHNIQUE 7: TRACKING THE COLORS OF THE MIND

This technique explains the thought and personality models in the form of color interpretation, just like color coding works as a memory mnemonic. Experts in this field suggest that the colors have a certain language in which they speak and exhibit their properties. These properties can be possessed by the bearer of that specific color and can have a great deal of influence over his personality and thought process. Even though several practices are already prevalent in this regard. Here we will try to customize this concept a bit to see what conclusions can we draw based on the color tracking technique.

When we set up a model or framework, it means that we are devising a common medium or mechanism for communication of thoughts and actions among the people. The colors of our mind are to be organized in a pattern or mechanism to be interpreted by whoever wants to read into our actions and thoughts. Penetrating deep into the thinking styles makes us aware of the motivations and objectives behind any action of an individual. This technique is a little unique in a way that the colors are universally used and understood yet symbolize different things everywhere. The behavior becomes a function in this technique, while colors are the tools to interpret that function. Experts compare them with ultra-violet rays to detect some "unseen" spectrum of the photograph.

These ultraviolet rays shine on the behavioral patterns and unveil the intricate thoughts behind each one of them. Another important quality of this model is, behaviors and actions become transferrable due to a common, vast medium of colors. The life disciplines such as education, business, marriage, etc. all are interlinked and mutually inclusive. An individual influenced by a specific color and exhibiting a prominent color in one of the disciplines, at some time, may become dominated by shades of other colors that are dominant in other disciplines. This transferability makes a person quite dynamic and flexible in nature which in turn makes him more successful. The working principle of the color mechanism is:

Connecting purposeful thinking to thoughtful action.

The aim of this technique is not just to realize the way a person thinks or attempts to complete a task but to realize the effect of that particular way of thinking on how he attempts to complete that task due to that particular thinking style. This is important so that one can adjust his thinking where it is necessary and develops an improved perception to attempt meaningful task completion. Also, this technique's purpose is not to fixate on a set thinking criteria or notion that you have tracked in yourself or someone else and tailor your actions accordingly but to understand the possible effects of each style and prepare yourself to use any of them per requirement. A sample color chart and mechanism researched by color psychologists, Sue Thame and Jerry Rhodes, is mentioned below for reference.

Follow these actions to understand this technique and implement it:

• Use the color chart or color-coded legend to track your score by selecting your responses to each action or thought according to your order of preference.

• Understand how people think by matching scores on these charts to know what they think.

• You can customize this chart to provide extended freedom to choose your chosen actions in order to relay the thinking style in a candid, unrestrained manner.

• Be quick and spontaneous in your selection and scoring; don't overthink. The truest response, revealing a person's real thoughts, is the quickest one.

• Don't reveal the color code before the charting in order to get the most accurate and uninfluenced results.

• Note that the score ranges from 0 to 10. In each unit, the maximum score could be 10 for three color-coded action prompts, collectively. For example, if you assign a 0 to the first choice, 3 to the second choice, then the third choice must get a score of 7 to complete the 10 marks quota.

• Know that the three major color domains are Red, Green, and, Blue. All the selected action prompt to track the responses will be falling under these three major color domains.

• The action prompts requiring preferred response selection will be categorized into units containing a collection of three actions receiving scores according to your preferred level. It will then be added to the score column of each color category to calculate which color domain gets a higher or lower score. (Note: Once you get the hang of it, you can later add more customized units.)

• Color interpretation will be revealed after the charting has been done, and the score has been calculated.

• A simple legend graphic is used as a key to distinguish which action or response belongs to which color category.

Sample Color Scoring Chart with Some Action Prompts

Unit 1	Score (0-10)
If you could choose the way to deal with a problem you would prefer to: a) Seek out an entirely new solution that surprises others, different from old ways. b) Stick to what seems right and rational. c) Reach a middle ground by opting for what is common and sensible, and what needs improvement.	....
Unit 2	
At the time of event planning, the best thing you like about it is: a)Getting to choose between complex yet exciting choices about what should be done. b)Imagining potentially negative outcomes and thinking positive alternatives beforehand. c)Organizing things, sorting them into lists, charts, etc., making preparations.	....
Unit 3	
The best method to shop is: a)Keeping my mind open when considering all choices and expecting a newer variety. b)Will be better if I know more about the available product choices before making a choice. c)Will never start until every detail and a list is made to follow systematically.	....

Thinking as a whole is a combination of three component colors; RGB (Red, Green, and Blue). These three aspects or dimensions define the mechanism of your thinking process as a whole, integrated concept. You should add each unit's a's, b's, and c's in separate columns as each action prompt stated in the chart above corresponds to a particular color domain. The added score after calculation should be mentioned in the score section of the table given below relative to the columns of colors that represent a distinctive personality trait or thinking category each. The score legend can be referred to understand the collective score in each category.

Color:	a) Green	b) Red	c) Blue
Score:	. . . . . .	. . . . . .	. . . . . .

Score & Color legend

(Note: The score legend may range from as low as 5 to as high as 70 and above; this will depend entirely on the number of units added in the chart and the number of action prompts' responses being tracked and scored.)

In this scenario, we have three units of action prompts

having a total of nine responses. Therefore, our customized sample score legend to determine the dominance of a particular color category or domain will be:

--> **0-5** = You probably avoid thinking in this sort of style. Mostly, this color may get overlooked by you to the point of neglect.

--> **5-10** = You may take this color as an alternative thinking style, i.e., "maybe this as well" sort of thinking.

--> **10-15** = You are able to think more often than not in this color style.

--> **15-20** = You are regularly led by this color domain. Your thoughts are highly motivated by this style.

--> **20 and above** = You tend to overuse this thinking style of color, weakening your potential to use other colors.

The meaning of the colors is the following:

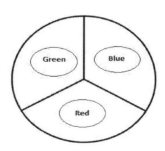

Red says: Describe what is True

Blue says: Judge what is Right

Green says: Realize what is New

Example of how to use this method

Take a pen and paper to write the results I will give you and to understand how to use this methodology.

The example consists of three units, each of the three units proposing three types of answers.

Each answer can be given a numerical score that starts from zero and goes up to 10. The value zero indicates that this action does not belong to you, and you would never do it; the value ten suggests that it is an action that you always do. For each unit, the sum of the scores of the three answers must be 10. For example, if on the answer a) I assigned the score five, to the answer B) I assigned the score three, consequently to the answer c) I will have to assign the score 2.

The meaning of the colors is the following:

Red says: Describe what is True

Blue says: Judge what is Right

Green says: Realize what is New

Now we begin to assign scores to the three units.

UNIT 1

Question: If you could choose to deal with a problem you would prefer to:

Answer a) Seek out entirely new solution that surprises others, different from old ways.

The Score is: 5

Answer b) Stick to what seems right and rational

The score is: 3

Answer c) Reach a middle ground by opting for what is common and sensible, and what needs improvement.

The score is: 2

UNIT 2

Question: At the time of event planning, the best thing you like about it is:

Answer a) How to choose between complex yet exciting choice about what should be done

The Score is: 3

Answer b) Imagining potentially negative features and thinking positive alternatives beforehand.

The score is: 5

Answer c) Organizing things, sorting them into list, charts, etc., making preparations

The score is: 2

UNIT 3

Question: The best method to shop is:

Answer a) Keeping my mind open when considering all choices and expecting a new variety

The Score is: 3

Answer b) Will be better if I know more about the available product choice before making a choice

The score is: 4

Answer c) Will never start until every detail and list is made to follow systematically

The score is: 3

The attribution of the scores of each unit is over. Now all the values of the answers a) of each of the three units must be added together, then all the values of the answers B) of each unit, and finally, all the answers C) of each unit.

The result is the following

Total score answer a): 11

Total score answer b): 12

Total score answer c): 7

The added score after calculation should be mentioned in the score section of the table given below relative to the columns of colors that represent a distinctive personality trait or thinking category each. The score legend can be referred to understand the collective score in each category.

The answer a) represents the color GREEN

The answer b) represents the color RED

The answer c) represents the BLUE color

In this example, we have a prevalence of the answer b), red color, with a score equal to twelve.

This means that you are able to think more often than not in this color style: Judge what is Right.

TECHNIQUE 8: DETECTING TANGIBLE & INTANGIBLE MOOD INFLUENCERS

A person can be categorized by his proactivity or reactivity. According to this technique, we will be discussing ways or signs to detect what ticks a person and how. Unlike the techniques in an initial couple of weeks, here the focus will be more on how rather than on why. People might disagree, but the truth is that the influence can be altered. The objects or emotions, and the thoughts or actions, which influence our mood, can be customized, changed, or blocked out completely on will.

"People are about just as happy as they make up their mind to be." - Lincoln A.

The choices we make determine our daily mood; the more proactive your choices are, the more contented you will feel. The more reactive you become, the more guilt and self-consciousness you will experience. Be a glass of calm water; don't be a bottle of fizzy drink that reacts readily the instance it is stimulated. The analysis of human behavior and personality lets you become more conscious of your own choices as well. While examining the level of proactiveness or reactiveness in your subject, you are likely to self-examine yourself too.

Consider some moods & behaviors as an example:

✓ Putting the blame on someone else is being reactive.

✓ Accepting your shortcomings and still trying to make amends is being proactive.

✓ Holding grudges and making not only others but your own self as well as being reactive.

✓ Forgiving others and your own self as well and adding a new page in life's book in order to move forward is being proactive.

However, not being affected by influencers and blocking them is one thing, while trying to control them is quite another entirely. Some influencers are tangible or physical objects or sensations that affect our state of mind and influence the mood. For e.g. hot weather, rain, rough clothes, cold food, dirty shoes, tangled hair, sweeteners, edible supplements, perfumes, traffic jam, stuffy room, loud noises and commotion, screeching, slapping or physical violence, kisses and hugs, handshakes, pat on the back, sunlight, airy space, warmth inducing material such as a fireplace, etc. Suppose, a person is easily ticked by a display of physical violence. He is sitting with you in a restaurant, talking, and you are observing him, and suddenly you detect a peculiar vibe coming off from his direction, altering his mood. He may seem to be put off by something, suppressing his anger or displeasure. If you are quick to record this mood change, the next step will be to discover how it happened. You look around or follow his direction of the sight to notice a boy being hit by his father in front of the public. You should be able to put two and two together to understand that your subject of analysis may be influenced by this display of violence.

However, if you were not reading this right now, you may have assumed his sudden mood change to be either because of something you did or said or because he just seems like that sort of a moody person who seems to have these unexpected mood swings, so no big deal.

Consider another example. Suppose you are expecting some guests. You have prepared the living room as a reception area. You have cleaned moderately and freshened the air with some sandalwood spray. Your guests come, and you greet and seat them. Upon greeting, you notice one person is not particularly responding. He has a look of distaste on his face and you are startled. You think hard to come up with possible mood-changing agents that could have dampened his mood, and you may realize that it may be due to the unusual fragrance or stuffiness of the room or maybe because of a headache that he has since morning. In all the possible situations, he has been compelled to act in a particular manner, not willingly so. You have to give a person the benefit of the doubt before making faulty assumptions.

Another type of mood influencers is intangible or emotional influencers that include feelings of gratitude, guilt, love, appreciation, nostalgia, etc. Closely related to motivational factors mentioned previously, the major difference between mood influencers and motivational factors is that motivation governs our thoughts and intentions while these thoughts turn into respective actions willingly and intentionally. The mood influencers are mostly the elements that alter our mood or actions unwillingly or unintentionally. While motivation is a need and requirement to perform a particular task, mood influencer is a compulsive agent to affect your train of thoughts, the direction of your response, and the path of your action resulting in often unplanned outcomes. Sometimes, however, people might willingly create an environment possessing desired mood influencers to accelerate the performance and achieve a planned outcome. In this way, the mood influencers act more or less like motivational factors to plan an action. For instance, a person likes to work in a spacious, sunny room with a fragrant atmosphere. He seems to work much better if space is clutter-free and clean. In this situation, he can use the mood influencers positively to enhance his performance. By drawing the curtains, letting the sunlight in, preferring to work in day hours, spraying his favorite scent or using an electric fragrance diffuser in the room, and minimizing the stuff, he may create an environment that lifts up his mood and enhances his work performance. The efforts made to ensure this is also a telling sign of his personality traits such as dedication to work, concentration, hard work, order and organization, and an aversion to mess.

Suppose, your friend may seem to be inattentive and unresponsive to your conversation. You might assume that he is just not interested in what you have to say or complain about. But maybe, at that time, he is more influenced by the huge pile of incomplete work that awaits him at home for which the deadline is nearing. Maybe this is the reason he is preoccupied at the moment, but it does not mean that he doesn't care about you. After all, a huge workload and short deadlines could be a mood dampener for sure. Keeping in mind these possible influencers, practice this technique to understand more about how moodiness shapes an individual's personality.

TECHNIQUE 9: DISCOVERING THE CLIFTON STRENGTHS

Clifton's strengths' concept has been proposed by the Father Of Strength Psychology, Don Clifton. According to the American Psychological Association (APA), through the invention of these strengths, psychology got a new perspective on the analysis of human personality. Regularly focusing on these strengths and their appearance in a person's personality makes speed-reading them easier and fun. However, a fact must be noted that the mere presence of these strengths may not provide a guarantee for achieving success in life. Research shows that an individual who pays closer attention to his strengths and utilizes them purposefully has higher chances of success and achievement. And those who do not avail of a chance to focus and utilize their strengths are the ones who late regret the lost opportunities in life and remain standing on the same step of the achievement ladder without much progress.

Over the past years, numerous people have attempted the strength-assessment just for the fun of it and without realizing the key purpose behind it. Business models, leadership tests, school exams, career counseling sessions, and psychological therapies, all of them have, in some way or other, make use of this assessment to analyze personalities and behavior models. This assessment can estimate the level of productivity used in both work and relationships. If you make use of these strengths and let others be aware of them as well, you may increase your chances of living in a far more productive environment than what you are experiencing now. You can also understand how Clifton Strengths define distinctive potentials in your personality that can transform in a kinematic manner if motivated appropriately. Another most important feature, apart from motivation, would be to acquire the necessary skills and knowledge about the strength or talent that you think you possess, or a person you are analyzing possesses. This is because, mere talent can get you nowhere if you or any other person possessing it, do not know how to use it properly in a constructive manner.

The working principle of strength psychology is to work and focus more on the already present strengths in a person rather than the absent ones. Because it so happens that we tend to focus more on our shortcomings and the lack or absence of certain strengths in our personalities. Striving to learn them, we tend to forget how to maximize our already present potential and gain expertise in a specific niche area. As a result, people usually have a superficial knowledge of several things but an in-depth understanding of not even one single area or domain.

Imagine the dilemma of people nowadays. All their lives, they have tried to become what they are not. It is almost like an occupational or psychological hazard. It happens to us as well. Whenever we realize that we have a fault in some areas, and it needs improvement, we automatically start paying more attention to it. This becomes so habitual to us that in our quest to achieve what we are not, or what we lack, we start neglecting what we already have. The ever-present inner qualities bestowed to us, if we take them for granted, they may start working against us instead of working in our favor.

Suppose, your son is quite an enthusiast when it comes to athletic activities. He always performs well in sports. He is, however, quite average when it comes to academics.

Whenever you get to see his poor performance report, you realize that he has been lacking in the academics and needs improvement in this area. You motivate him to take remedial classes or enhancement courses, etc. He starts paying more attention to the academics side despite craving for athletic activities. A time comes when he may become above average in academics, but lack of sports practice may transform his excellent performance into a below-average strength or capacity in his much-loved area. An appropriate analysis is needed to understand which strengths are present in a person and why they should be retained and polished even more.

Research has shown that although we, humans, are creatures possessing adaptability, some traits remain stable, lying there, in our personality core. They are not much affected by time, mood change, or other influential factors such as our passions, interests, talents, etc. Clifton Strength finder attempts to assess these sorts of more stable strengths present in the people.

Experts suggest that people who start with raw talent and

follow it with necessary investment, knowledge, skills, professional training and expertise actually multiply their chances of success and productivity, effectively reducing the chances of time wastage and extra hard work, overly struggling to achieve little or no return. Therefore, sooner than later, people must discover their strengths and team them up with all the right elements to make a perfect recipe for strength and success. As an analyzer of people and their personality, you must realize the ground fact that,

---

"Every individual has talents and strengths, just waiting to be unearthed from the garden soil of their personality." --
I F.

The strength finding assessment does not aim to supply people with strengths they want to acquire, but help in locating your areas of potential talents and latent strengths or abilities. The following are the famous 34 Clifton strengths found in people. These strengths are listed in alphabetic order:

1. Achiever: A constant inner drive to achieve. This strength motivates you to have an achievement every day,

however small it may seem, in order to feel a sense of accomplishment and satisfaction.

2. Activator: A person has this strength if he is constantly looking for some action and active participation in a task. You would have often heard some team members of a project asking, "When can the work be started?" or "Shall we go ahead then?". Once a task has been planned, they carve for some prompt action.

3. Adaptability: This one is a present-day man. Always adjusting and living in the moment. He is able to respond willingly and adapt according to the situational demands despite having made prior plans.

4. Analytical: This person is constantly presenting others with challenging concepts to prove, show, exemplify, etc., the facts and scenarios. This person is quite objective and not easily swayed by emotions. He remains steadfast in his opinions and continues searching for ground realities to understand the possible relationship between facts and judgments.

5.   Arranger: This means an individual is able to conduct and manage several simple and complex things in an organized manner and enjoys finding the best way to do so.

6.   Belief: This person has a strong sense of altruism, righteousness, a general love for spirituality, strong moral conduct, and a fixed belief system that has enduring values which he follows in every walk of life.

7.   Command: It makes a person take charge and control other people and situations. The person possessing this strength often imposes his views and commands others. He has a confident persona and doesn't hesitate to confront and take risks.

8.   Communication: This person loves to speak, write, host, and present. He likes to be in contact with the public in one way or another. He is often seen narrating past memories, stories, and life incidents in social gatherings to extend people's attention span and divert it towards him.

9.   Competition: This person's sense of achievement is

always dependent on the rate of other people's success. He is compelled to compare and outperform his peers to feel more successful. He thrives for the challenging win and the excitement that comes with it.

10. Connectedness: This individual sees the world as an integrated sphere. Each person is linked to another; every action relates to a cause or motive. This person knows about how closely linked humans living in a society are and the mutual responsibilities that come with this connection.

11. Consistency: This means believing in quality and regularity over quantity and sporadicity. Balance is this person's principle. He tends to maintain fairness in every relation and work objective.

12. Context: This person lives in the present by relating it to the past. He uses his prerequisite knowledge of past experiences to understand present questions and situations.

13. Deliberative: Vigilance, carefulness, privacy, cautiousness, and a reserved attitude just about sums up this

strength.

14. Developer: This person is always looking for hidden potentials and talents in other people. He is someone who enjoys facilitating further development of these potentials by his speech, actions, and guidance. He takes each human being as a work in progress, exploring and thriving on possible chances of further growth and improvement.

15. Discipline: He is a predictable individual needing an orderly life. He needs everything to be planned ahead of time in order to avoid physical disturbance or mental chaos.

16. Empathy: This person has an inbuilt radar to sense the emotions and feelings of those around him.

17. Focus: The one driven by this talent needs a clear goal to strive for. He needs to set his priorities straight to help him focus on which path should be taken in life to achieve his goal.

18. Futuristic: This person likes to look ahead in the

direction of the future, trying to foresee his life after the present has become the past.

19. Harmony: Harmony means the person believes in the goodness of a conflict-free environment. He is quite agreeable. He likes to settle an arising conflict by reach mutual agreement and maintaining a harmonized environment.

20. Ideation: This one is a brainstormer, an innovator, and an idea generator. He is readily fascinated by ideas and their connections to things, tasks, and people.

21. Includer: "Make room for others too." The person working by this philosophy is likely to be an Includer. He is accepting a person, welcoming as many people in his circle as possible to not make them feel left out. He believes in equal opportunities.

22. Individualization: More or less an antonym for inclusiveness, the person having this strength tends to detect the individual qualities of the people. He does not like to

generalize people, hates stereotypes, and generic groups that overshadow the individual potential of a person.

23. Input: This person likes to investigate and search for answers. He likes to gather information, interesting things like coins, books, pictures, etc. Each action is done to have an input, i.e., knowledge and a new perspective on something, someplace, or some person. This individual is curious about the world, as though he was the computer seeking input from peripheral devices such as sensory organs and environmental factors, etc.

24. Intellection: An intellectual likes to think and function through cognitive activities that exercise the brain.

25. Learner: This person is a seeker of knowledge. He derives excitement and thrill from the process of gaining knowledge and the prospect of being able to comprehend things.

26. Maximizer: He is a perfectionist. An excellence-seeker. He does not care for below average results. He

targets optimum performance.

27. Positivity: This person is optimistic and generous. He is looking at the pros rather than the cons in a given situation.

28. Realtor: This person has a close-knit circle of friends and family in whose company he feels contented. He may not exhibit shyness in meeting new people, he might even enjoy it sometimes due to certain reasons, but he still prefers to be closer to his loved ones and be in familiar company.

29. Responsibility: The responsible person always takes ownership of his commitments and duties. He feels morally and emotionally obliged on his own accord, to fulfill his promises and roles honorably. He has a sense of integrity and feels bound to compensate if, in case, he could not deliver on a promise.

30. Restorative: This person thrives to restore the damages that have been done. He takes on challenging problems and comes up with solutions. While other people make mistakes and run away from making up for them or

correcting them. He sets the problem straight and puts the situation right by seeking the root cause of trouble, conceptualizing the solution, and implementing it.

31. Self-Assurance: This person has faith in his abilities. He has a "can-do" attitude. This means that an individual not only has confidence in his potential strengths but also in his judgment.

32. Significance: This person strives to be recognized for his abilities and hard work. Given significant importance to his abilities makes him feeling more energized and appreciated. He likes to stand out from the crowd in a noticeable stance.

33. Strategic: Sorting through the various themes and choices, and reaching the best method to implement, is what strategic person does.

34. Woo: This one is a public pleaser. People are easily won over by him due to his likable personality, whether they are strangers or not.

CHAPTER 6

COMMUNICATION AND PERSONALITY

C ommunication is the process of sharing. It has derived from the Latin word "communico." When two or more persons meet, they share information, feelings, ideas, thoughts, etc. Communication is a continuous process of speaking listening and understanding. Communication is a skill. Most people are born with the physical ability to talk, but to speak well and coherently, one must have to adapt certain key characteristics to make his communication skills perfect. Good communication skills build your personality. It gives you confidence and boosts your self-esteem thus giving your personality a sober and sophisticated look.

Communication is the most vital means by which people are connected in society, and a lack of good communicational skills can make society a miserable place to live. So, for living in a peaceful environment, its necessary that man should have good communication skills. Today, the most successful person is the one who can communicate effectively. Good communication build strong personalities, and strong personalities make great decisions. It's the skill a man develops until the day he dies. There is no limit to developing and improving this specific skill. Humans must keep moving and trying to improve their personalities further with proper communication techniques. Remember, we are here judging their methods to communicate rather than their skills in effective communication. You would be analyzing people this week by the way they communicate.

Nonverbal Communication

Another important element of communication is nonverbal communication. Nonverbal communication is interpersonal communication with linguistic means. The non-verbal message conveys feelings more accurately than those of verbal means. The non-verbal communication process comprises of several factors like appearance, facial expressions, eye contact, gestures, touch, postures, voice, space, and time. Nonverbal communication is everything except words. When it comes to appearance, your personality speaks itself. A person's personality appearance can affect the impressions others receive of his credibility, honesty, competence, judgment, or status.

A person's face is more capable of communicating nonverbally than other parts of the human body. The face sends messages about his emotions like happiness, sorrow, frustration, fear, etc. In fact, we don't have to ask people about their feelings. Their facial expressions reveal their present emotional state. Similarly, when it comes to effective nonverbal communication, eye contact is the main factor in reflecting one's intention through his eye movements. Direct eye contact shows the confidence level, whereas the breaking of eye contact gives the signals of shyness to other people.

You can predict a person's intentions just by the gestures he is showing. For example, nail-biting shows the nervousness of a person, nodding head shows agreement, and a thumbs-up signal is used to show appreciation. This is how people communicate with gestures without even saying a single word. Though the communication is nonverbal, the exclamatory sounds coming from a person's mouth can transfer the message he wants to deliver. For instance, if he has gotten hurt accidentally, an "ouch" sound comes from his mouth, which shows his pain or discomfort. Likewise, if he is in a sorrowful mood or feeling melancholic, he sighs, which communicates his sad emotions.

These factors make nonverbal communication strong and powerful. One cannot deny the role of gestures, eye contact, facial expressions, and other similar cues that help in effective nonverbal communication. It is a built-in natural instinct in living beings to communicate. When language was not there, still people managed to communicate with each other through different body gestures and postures or even graphical symbols. Effective communication is important whether it is verbal or nonverbal, and the intentions are a vital part of all the means of communication. During your analysis, when you observe the person communicating something verbally or nonverbally, you must look for possible answers to the questionable intentions of your subject.

Week 3

TECHNIQUE 10: SPOT THE BODY LANGUAGE (GESTURES, STANCE, POSTURE, ETC.)

This one is the most important aspect of nonverbal communication and is relatively easier to detect. When a person stops speaking, the body starts communicating. The focus of the audience is directed towards each hand gesture that is portrayed, and each posture that the body represents. The stance is also important to notice in people who are mostly moving about or standing nearby, such as in the queues or at restaurant counters, etc. The following are four body postures that may be attributed to certain personality traits.

•   A person standing with a straight back. This is a neutral posture depicting a calm, assured manner of behavior.

•   A person maintaining leaning forward in a collapsing posture. It reveals the giving up attitude or depressed mood of a person.

•   A person maintaining an upright position with spread

arms and feet wide apart. This often exhibits a confident, open-minded attitude with a dominant stance.

- A person slightly inclining toward the other person while standing beside him. This represents a sweetly sympathetic gesture. For example, a teacher leans towards his student while listening to him.

While analyzing a personality, it must be noted that the interpretation of these gestures or postures is still quite subjective in nature despite being researched time and again. This is because humans often display unpredictable, sudden responses, yet in the long run, these patterns may become predictably repetitive due to observation and consistent analysis. Therefore, once you start practicing, you will begin to predict the expected responses of your subject or even guess their alternatives in a given situation.

TECHNIQUE 11: PERCEIVE THE EYE MOVEMENT

They say that eyes are sort of windows to the human soul. How much correct depends on the keenness of the beholder during his observation. Each glance matters, and each movement is recorded by the serious individual dedicated to learning this technique of analyzing people. There can be definite relativity between eye movement and cognitive activity as described by the famous psychologist William James.

Consider these points when observing eye movements:

1. Pupil dilation usually means attraction and interest in the percieved person.

2. There are 6 specific eye movements in the generalized version of the theory. VR, VC, AR, AC, AD, and K.

   o VR (Visually remembered): Directed to the upper left

     ▪ remembering images previously seen

   o VC (Visually constructive): Directed to the left

side

- creating images haven't seen before

o AR (Auditively remembered): Directed to the lower left

- remembering images previously heard

o AC (Auditively constructive): Directed to the upper right

- creating sounds or voices that haven't been heard before by you. For e.g. , upcoming viva questions by the examiner.

o AD (Digitally Auditive): Directed to the right side

- focusing on the voice of internal dialogue

o K (Kineasthetic): Directed to the lower right

- the eyes are focusing on sensory perception, bodily sensations, and experiencing emotions such as the feel of ice melting on the hand.

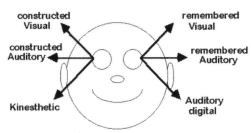

TECHNIQUE 12: READ THE FACIAL EXPRESSIONS

The face holds the main emotions and expressions of a person. Being the center of attraction and observation, it can convey numerous meaningful signs to communicate a particular message. If verbal communication is not paired with appropriate facial expressions, the words become quite meaningless. On the other hand, even if the person remains silent, the facial expression or his gestures can say it all. That is why the pantomime has become such an effective presentation method. The facial expressions are the responses stimulated by mood, thoughts, and the surrounding environment of a person. If he is angry due to disturbing noise, his face will portray his displeasure, and if he is listening to a melancholic sound of a prayer, his expression may become wistful. The strong facial expressions may carry a kind of power in them, intimidating others or letting them become apprehensive such as looking into an interviewer's confidently strong face may confuse a job applicant for a while.

You will have to learn this technique to ensure you know what their faces show!

TECHNIQUE 13: CHECK THE HANDWRITING AND DOODLING

The handwriting of a person is a strong indicator of his state of mind. For a great observer, keen on subtle signs that reflect an individual's personality, pen or pencil strokes on the surface of a paper becomes a medium of silent communication. These strokes and marks define how a person is feeling. Lazy doodling appearing almost as an illegible script symbolizes the instability of emotions. Whereas, strong strokes with a purposeful grip on the pencil tells us about the clear-headed state of the writer's mind.

Too much pressure exerted on the writing tool while writing may also reveal the passionate nature of the person. There is a whole new branch of psychological sciences called Graphology which deals with the personality analysis of individuals by judging their handwriting. US National Pen Company states that there may be more than 5000 personality traits revealed just by interpreting the dynamics of a person's handwriting style. Factors such as spacing, letter-size, the particular shape of individual letters, pen pressure, etc. are determinants in this regard.

TECHNIQUE 14: CHECK THE PREFERRED COLOR OF CLOTHES

The colors are also powerful mood influencers and personality indicators. The famous profiling system called true colors is based on their effects on the person's strengths and shortcomings and their further enhancement. For instance, the green personality type is often more loyal than others, while the orange one is less passionate and calmer than the red one. Wearing these colors according to the order of preference describes the nature of that individual and matching his actions with the prescribed color traits might describe the reason for his choice in the long run.

TECHNIQUE 15: NOTICE THE SILENCE AND SMILE

They say silence is more powerful than speech. Once a person becomes silent, his inner personality starts emitting vibes that attract the focus of a person keenly observing him. It is like the soul of a silent person is calling people to come read its feelings and emotions. Some people prefer to remain silent throughout the conversation and only smile at appropriate times to denote a required response. This means that they prefer to actively listen and comprehend your words, instead of interrupting you. It also can mean that these people are wiser than most people because they measure their words well and cherish them. You would see that when eventually they decide to speak, their concise words contain a wealth 0f sensible advice and actionable wisdom which they learned through silently listening and contemplating.

TECHNIQUE 16: RECORD THE RESPONSES TO CERTAIN STIMULI

The environment is your stimulator. It contains sensory diodes to trigger the thought process. A study conducted in the past suggested a technique called DTR, i.e., Disrupt than refrain to stimulate people by showing them tantalizing call-to-action scenarios or procedures. You can follow this technique by noticing how people get influenced by words or actions if arrange in a peculiarly different manner or sequence.

For, e.g., some people might believe $299 to be way cheaper than $300 at first glance. This is called confusing the waters or playing with the psyche. Similarly, notice how people often react when told about time in terms of minutes instead of hours. It makes their brain perplexed while processing the concept of time in less frequent terms, and therefore, helps the simulator to achieve the desired response. Observe the stimuli projected in front of people and record their way of reactions in this sort of situation. Another sort of active stimulus in the surroundings to trigger the desired response in people would be to hang a large pair of eyes in a public area such as a park or restaurant, for instance. This will make people have a psychological response in their conscience. They will be more careful to follow the rules of that particular place like avoid littering the place, etc.

Week 4

CHAPTER 7

VERBAL COMMUNICATION

N o communication is completed until the message is received by the receiver. And to make sure that the message has been reached to the specific person properly, people strive to find better ways to reach their audience as the message must have to be communicated in a proper manner. In communication, a principle of sharing is evident. But this sharing needs appropriate verbal communication techniques. A person's personality gets doomed when they open their mouths, and insignificant words come out. It needs proper work and time to enhance and improve an individual's verbal communication skills. No one is born perfect. But people work hard to achieve perfection. Experts believe that good verbal skills are important for your carrier, relationships, and self-esteem.

Verbal communication plays a powerful role in the enhancement of one's personality, career development, and happy personal life. We all are bound directly or indirectly with each other as we move along together in a society. We need to communicate at every step of our lives. We need words to define emotions, thoughts, objects, and behaviors. But these are not just words; these are the verbal skills we learn by the passage of time and with people from whom we interact. Similarly, the person you are going to analyze will also be communicating using more or less the same skills and methods for the same goals and purposes. Thus, understanding them becomes easier.

Pretext Communication

Pretext communication is dodging another person in a

manner that he realizes the real reason for some specific act later. It is about misinterpreting or hiding information. For example, Anna called her friend on a sleepover without giving her a hint that she wants to complete her homework with her.

Contextual communication

It is the form of communication in which both parties know about the exchange of information on account of cultural, environmental, and relational contexts. To explain it better, consider an example of Bluetooth or mobile verification process. When we use mobiles, we have to go through biometrics or personal information sharing, and both sides know the input and output of the shared information. This is called contextual communication.

Sub-textual Communication

The subtext is an underlying emotion or intention. It lies behind the actual communication acting like an unspoken dialogue amidst the spoken words. As communication experts say that a person's voice is a vehicle carrying several passengers such as emotions, intonations, and pretexts, and subtexts. Suppose, you are hearing a person delivering a speech about flood victims in a charity fundraiser. You hear him speak seemingly practical words, but his voice carries an underlying sympathy and care for the cause. This behind the curtain's emotion is a sub-textual part of an otherwise ordinary conversation. Similarly, you often find yourself saying "Don't worry, I am fine" with an angry tone, to a nagging friend who keeps on asking if you are okay. When in reality, your voice suggests your anger and sadness and defies your actual words. The art of analyzing people through their communication styles makes you quickly realize these underlying intonations and understand the real intention of a person regardless of what his words are. You may have heard, actions speak louder than words, but here actually, the tone is far more revealing than the word itself.

Intertextual Communication

Even though, according to popular opinion, intertextuality means the explanation of one text in terms of another text or exploring the interrelationship of similar textual pieces. Here, in terms of communication, intertext means to relate the saying or communicative expression of a person to another one that he or she or some other person said or expressed. This way, a person's thoughts, and uttered expressions can be defined and explained through references in a relative manner. The metaphors, quotations, or allusions are sometimes used as intertextual devices. People often communicate in an intertextual manner when they attempt to cite another author or person's sayings to relate to their opinions or statements.

The role of verbal skills is very significant and important as we cannot stay mute for hours. We need to share. We need to communicate; we need to interact for the reason of survival. Man cannot survive without letting out the thoughts, feelings, and emotions. And this can only be possible with coherent and concise verbal communications. There are some barriers also which affect verbal communication such as distractions, lack of interest, emotional barriers, the difference in point of view, physical disabilities like hearing problems, speech difficulties, etc. These can be the cause of ineffective verbal communication. The most important barrier is the linguistic barrier as will be discussed below.

Types of Communication Barriers

As mentioned earlier, interpersonal communication may fail because of different communication barriers. An emotionally intelligent person strives to learn empathy by overcoming barriers in communication. This individual tries to learn methods of effective communication by analyzing another person's way of communication; therefore, he must understand that sometimes, these barriers are unavoidable. Obstacles such as distortion or disturbance during a conversation, a disturbed state of mind, or moodiness may become the cause of miscommunication among individuals. Due to these factors, the chances of misunderstandings increase exponentially during communication, and this results in a lack of successful comprehension of the transmitted message.

Communication barriers may vary in nature. Some of them are psychological, linguistic, physical, cultural, emotional, etc. See the details of these barriers below:

1. Linguistic Barriers

The main one is the language barrier that can affect

effective communication. Language is an essential communication tool. Every state has its specific language and a thick dialect. If you are unaware of the language or dialect of a region, it can make communication nearly impossible in some cases. Nor can a person being unaware of the language of another individual be able to analyze his voice intonation or verbal expressions.

2. Psychological Barriers

Several psychological and mental issues can disturb effective communication. These issues may vary in people, such as speech disorders, stage fear, depression, phobia, etc. Sometimes, it can be challenging to manage these conditions.

3. Emotional Barriers

Your emotional IQ determines the comfort and ease of communication. An emotionally mature person can communicate effectively. For effective communication, you will need a perfect blend of facts and emotions. Particular emotions like humor, sadness, fear, frustration, and anger may blur your executive capacities.

4. Physical Barriers

Physical barriers are represented by closed doors or cabins, noise, faulty equipment (used for communication), etc. You can remove these barriers easily by using alternatives to facilitate effective communication. Sometimes, physical separation between numerous employees and dependency on some defective equipment for communication can decrease the effectiveness of the mutual interface.

5. Cultural Barriers

The world is becoming globalized; therefore, a large office often contains people from different regions of the world. Remember, the meaning of a word can be different in every culture. Drinks, food, pets, and general behavior may vary drastically in each culture.

For effective communication, you have to consider different cultures during a conversation. Companies may offer specialized courses at their orientation stages. The purpose of these courses is to teach tolerance and courtesy to people from different cultures. In order to be efficient in reading people's behavior and approaching them with the right attitude without causing an offense intentionally or unintentionally, you have to identify and address these communication barriers appropriately.

TECHNIQUE 17: NOTE THE GREETING & FAREWELL

The conversation your subject is having will have an opening and an end. This technique lets you focus on the way he opens the conversation with people by greeting them and the way he closes it by saying his farewell. You would have to focus on his style of greeting his guests, host, or appointed help in the office environment.

• Note, does he say "Hi, what's up!" or "Hey/Hello" in a conversational, candid manner or "Good Evening / Good day to you, etc." in a stiff tone? The former will let you know his informal and friendly personality while the latter may suggest a bit more formal and reserved attitude. The excitement, pent up anticipation, and overwhelming joy can also be conveyed through the warmth of the greeting, whereas the suppressed annoyance or displeasure on seeing someone unexpected or unwelcomed can be revealed through the cold, distant greeting message.

• Similarly, notice how he quotes his farewell message.

A person who is quite reluctant to leave someone's precious company will often be regretful while saying his farewell. His words would portray his eagerness to meet again, such as "Can't wait to see you again soon." While a person finding another's company boring or offensive will be impatient to take his leave. His parting words may reveal how glad he is to finally have the chance to escape such as "I think I should go now as I have something quite important to attend to, excuse me."

TECHNIQUE 18: NOTE THE CONVERSATION IN BETWEEN

The research shows how often people tend to overwhelm their audience by wordy phrases and nonstop banter. It sometimes shows that with an unfavorable audience, people fill their conversational address with continuous verbal messages that are complicated to be processed quickly by the brain. This way, the chances of any disapproval are lessened, and an expected argument can be avoided. Diverting the conversation to a person's favorite topic can also grab his interest. A person showing extra quietness or responding with hmms and aahs can also be deemed uninterested or preoccupied.

TECHNIQUE 19: READ BETWEEN THE LINES (UNDERSTAND THE INNUENDOS)

The popular "Inneundo Effect" suggests that people can be saying something positive and another, less positive thing can be inferred from their words. The fact is that you must learn this technique if you want to understand what people say and what they really think or intend to do. An open mind and an observing eye can notice numerous things. Try to read between the lines as merely visible text interpretation might not be enough while analyzing people and speed-reading their minds.

While your subject may seem quite disinterested in buying a particular book, he may be fixated on some alternative approach such as listening to a program on the same topic instead. He may say, "Interesting topic it is, but I am not buying that book, you do that. I am not that much into reading complex books. I prefer spending my time listening to radio programs."

Even if he has not clearly declared that he wants to know more about the topic, he has expressed that he thinks it to be interesting. He has also stated that he is more into listening to the radio than reading complex books. But he hasn't declared the topic to be complex, just the format of its presentation. This means that he may be finding alternative ways to search and know more about the topic that he too has found interesting. Thus, as a person analyzing him, you may understand him more if you read between the lines of this conversation, not just the words that have clearly been said, but also the words that were just insinuated or implied.

TECHNIQUE 20: UNDERSTAND THE LANGUAGE AND SPEECH DEVICES

This technique focuses on learning the language of the person you are analyzing and the popular literary devices used in that particular language. Metaphors, similes, analogies, allusions, anagrams, amplification, anecdotes, anthropomorphism, allegory, euphemism, etc.

TECHNIQUE 21: LEARN TO DIFFERENTIATE BETWEEN HUMOR, SATIRE, AND PUN, ETC.

Sometimes, due to lack of awareness and skills, a joke is often taken too seriously, or a serious statement is often judged as bad humor. This can become a hindrance to the understanding of the general public. To learn this technique, you will have to study the difference between humor, satire, and pun, etc.

Humor: Anything that can provoke a laughing response or stimulate a smile.

Satire: Anything that is used to express irony, ridicule, scorn, or mockery of a particular concept or belief. It uses humor and exaggeration as one of the methods.

Pun: Intended for amusement purpose, it is a figure of speech. Used as a wordplay to induce multiple meanings or using homophones in a rhetorical or humorous sense.

TECHNIQUE 22: NOTICE THE EMPHASIS ON CERTAIN SPOKEN WORDS BY THE SPEAKER

The stress on certain words can reveal their importance in the voice of the communicator.

- Listen carefully.

- Notice the way the speaker is uttering or articulating each word.

- Notice his facial expression and concentration while he emphasizes on particular words or syllables of a word.

TECHNIQUE 23: NOTICE THE EMOTIONS AND WAY OF DIALOGUE DELIVERY MORE THAN THE WORDS

The expressions convey way more emotions than unfeeling words. You may consider a person cold because of his distant or reserved personality, but before you make an opinion about him, you must;

•   Look into the expressions and feel the undercurrent's emotions and feelings of a person rather than just paying attention to his dialogue.

•   Instead of just hearing what he delivers, see how he delivers it.

•   Notice how his throat may clog up while speaking brief, courteous words, due to the depth of his emotions.

TECHNIQUE 24: OBSERVE HOW THE SPEAKER IS RESPONDING TO CRITICISM, DISAGREEMENT, AND CONFRONTING STATEMENTS WHILE BEING ENGAGED IN A CONVERSATION

Through practicing this technique, an important aspect of your subject can be revealed. In the face of disapproval and while being confronted with disagreement, people often lose their cool.

• A person ready to accept his mistakes and reflect on them in order to improve himself will confront the disagreement in an agreeable manner.

• While a person thinking himself to be always right can be stubborn and never comfortable or cool while responding to even constructive criticism, he will try to start the blame game instead.

TECHNIQUE 25: OBSERVE HOW AN INDIVIDUAL IS RESPONDING TO APPLAUSE AND COMPLIMENTS

This technique involves noticing an individual at the time of receiving compliments and being praised. The one who is full of himself, showing signs of narcissism, may accept this praise as his birthright and take it for granted. However, the one having a modest behavior, moderate thoughts, and a grateful personality takes each compliment as a motivation to work harder and improve himself further. The one who does not lose his mind over constant applause and remains focused on his goals is the truly successful person. You would see how people get swayed by praise and forget how to be thankful. For e.g., team leaders often take all the credit for the success of a project forgetting to include their team members who have huge behind-the-scene efforts and hard work to their credit.

CHAPTER 8

ART OF PERSUASION AND INFLUENCING PEOPLE

You often have heard people making complaints about the communication gap or their inability to convince people effectively. Remember, your ability to influence and persuade people to get the things as per your desire depends upon your way of addressing them and your overall persona. In order to be better capable of making the environment to sing to your tune and people to walk your talk, you have to learn the ways to persuade people, to earn their respect, and get the support of your customers, coworkers, bosses, friends, and colleagues, etc.

Numerous people don't know that human communication involves a complicated process of influence and persuasion. For this reason, they are the ones being often persuaded to assist others instead of influencing people to support them. Personal will power and inner strengths can make you a persuasion expert. With your personal powers of confidence, self-belief, steadfastness, and a strong tone of voice, you can get your message across to your audience. You would have often seen how public speakers strategize their speeches and describe actionable pieces of advice to motivate their listeners. You can analyze that most of them derive these meaningful bits of advice and suggestions from their life experiences. They describe real-life examples to reach the masses and get them to relate easily to what they are saying.

Week 5

Motivation is key to persuasion. Each human action needs some motivation. If you want to analyze how a strong motivational speaker successfully influences his audience and convinces them, make sure to find out whether he is addressing them through mood influencers or motivational factors. People can be motivated by fear of failure and desire for profit. Make sure to work on these motivational factors to get desired results. The speakers often address these issues by stating relatable examples so that people actually feel compelled to respond to the call of action. There is also a famous mirror effect that depicts how people tend to subtly imitate other people in their way of speaking, and body gestures, etc. to project a feeling of familiarity and get their approval. Below are the actionable steps to summarize how to understand the art of influencing people through motivation and persuasion.

TECHNIQUE 26: LISTEN TO PUBLIC MOTIVATIONAL SPEAKERS

The best way of getting inspiration is by listening to motivational speeches.

✓ Pay attention to the actions, communication style, and body language of motivational speakers. These people can help you to develop your own communication style.

✓ Listen to the motivational speakers telling about real-life anecdotes combined with wisdom and experience.

✓ See how they interact with a group of people to stimulate their desire to achieve personal goals. With positive advice and anecdotes, it will be easy for you to analyze how people deal with pitfalls and failures of life.

TECHNIQUE 27: NOTICE PERSUASIVE STYLES IN MONOLOGUE AND DIALOGUE

Dialogue and monologue are literary devices in speeches. Monologue means the delivery of a speech by a character to express his feelings and thoughts to other characters. Dialogues are conversations between different characters. Remember, monologue refers to a lecture or speech delivered by one person only. Dialogue means a conversation between 2 to 3 or even more people. For instance, a TV show, talk show, or influential forum, etc.

You can reveal your inner character through monologue. If you want to address a crowd, you have to work on your monologue. For a conversation between 2 or more characters, it is essential to improve your dialogue. Remember, dialogue may portray the interaction style of a character. You can reveal your ideas and thoughts through dialogues. You will need an energetic style for your dialogue and monologue.

If you want to become an influential speaker, you have to work on your monologue and dialogue. It can be done through motivational speeches and talk shows. Listen to their speaking style and practice these skills in front of others. You can't become an influential executive without persuasive dialogue and monologue. To become a perfect speaker, start practicing in front of your friends and family members.

TECHNIQUE 28: OBSERVE THE WAY PEOPLE DEAL WITH THEIR SUBORDINATES

Active dealing with people is necessary for your workplace. With persuasive communication skills, dealing with workers and colleagues can be both a challenge and a joy. You must have the ability to deal with people in the workplace. For this reason, observe other employers and notice their way to deal with their subordinates.

It is essential to demonstrate a certain level of respect and consideration for people in the workplace or social circles. Along with respect, trust is a cornerstone when communicating with people. Faith becomes the foundation of positive communication, employee motivation, and interpersonal skill. To become an influential speaker, you have to practice active listening skills.

Do you want to get feedback from other people about your work? Make it easy with your body language and behavior. If you're going to become a persuasive speaker or analyze one who already is, feedback is necessary for both. Feedback permits you to adjust your style in dealing with people, challenges, and situations at work.

As a boss, you are responsible for communicating with your employees, coworkers, and colleagues. With your communication skills and gesture, you must tell them that you value their contribution to your business. It is a powerful way to influence people to follow your directions. They will be ready to work in your favor.

TECHNIQUE 29: OBSERVE THE WAY THEY RESPOND TO THEIR BOSS

For successful business operations, cooperate communication is a crucial element. Interacting with top-level management can be a real challenge. If you want to become an influential speaker, you have to notice the response of motivational speakers to their bosses. People often get intimidated by their employers upon meeting them. This often happens with new employees.

Boss and employees should be in a certain comfort zone; for this reason, they have to spend time to get familiar with each other. This may happen through short appraisal meetings, interviews, etc. A middle manager can interact with juniors more frequently and pass on the essential employee details to the boss. Some people to stay in touch with their bosses through middle management. Some people regard communication with their boss mildly challenging yet compete for it too, like a game of friendly chess. They feel compelled to stay ahead of their colleagues.

Consider yourself to be the person you are analyzing. How would you behave around your boss? A good employee always anticipates the needs of his/her boss. As an employee, paying attention to the working style and habits of your boss is important too. This helps improve your communication skills and job performance. You must have the ability to identify potential problems and offer possible solutions.

Notice the personality style and approach of both the boss and his employee. Their work relationship will help you understand their behavior model. If the boss likes to communicate over the phone instead of email, Employees often adjust and fine-tune their verbal communication skills. Some employees strictly follow the rule of sticking to business. They feel that there is no need to become friendly with their boss, indulging in personal conversations. Instead, their seriousness to work directs them to believe that the job needs a genuine interest in all things professional in contrast to personal bonding.

TECHNIQUE 30: OBSERVE THE WAY THEY COMMUNICATE AND WORK WITH THEIR PEERS AND FAMILY

Focus on others when they talk and work with their peers and family. Excellent communication skills are always required to create successful relationships with peers and family. Active listening is necessary to understand others and tell them that you always value their feedback.

✓ Observe. Do people pay attention to others' opinions and statements? How much they care and value their thoughts?

✓ Observe. Are they more comfortable in a familiar company than they were in the work environment or more professional climate?

✓ Observe and analyze your findings and match the results with the personality models to understand which category a person may belong to.

✓ Some people do follow effective techniques of communication. They make eye contact, move, or turn toward their conversation partner and a nod to their ideas. They try to ignore all possible distractions to increase their focus on their partner. These people are considered good listeners and considerate confidants among their peers and family.

Paying attention to the feelings and content behind each spoken word, they try to understand where their friends are coming from. Some people even exhibit the ability to understand emotions like anger, excitement, sadness, and joy through people's body language. This shows their keenness and excellent observational skills as well as their interest in others. A person full of himself, always talking, and making others listen may not be able to spare the chance of noticing these delicate nuances that define people and their personalities. Don't be that sort of a person and practice the art of becoming emotionally intelligent.

CHAPTER 9

CONFLICT RESOLUTION AND HUMAN BEHAVIOR

T he conflict resolution is an important and integral requirement within different aspects of real life. The human-specific behavior, in connection with the conflict-oriented situations and the specific response to them, is based on experience as well as the understanding of individuals in connection with conflicts. There is a possibility of different conflicts you come across the life of the individuals. The conflicting situations can usually arise when one person or group would start to emphasize on the fact that its interests are undermined. The nature and the complexity of the conflict can depend upon the understanding level as well as the human-specific behavior responding to that particular conflict-oriented environment.

A better understanding of the environment, as well as an exploration of different possibilities to resolve a particular problem and the conflict, can be productive for the people and the organizations. This helps them manage conflicting situations in a better way.

The human-specific behavior, in response to a particular conflict, has to be focused on the fact to understand the conflict in the first place. It is important for individuals and human beings getting into a conflicting situation to give the maximum level of the time for developing a better understanding of the different stances and points of view related to the conflict. The mutually agreeable place and time discuss the details of the conflict-oriented situation with respect to developing a better understanding of its dynamics and can play a positive and constructive role in its resolution. Each of the individual companies in the conflict-oriented situation has to come out to express its understanding as well as point of view about the conflict-oriented situation. It becomes significantly important for human beings to try to focus on the development of a better understanding of ideas and thinking of other people who are involved in a particular country.

The patience to hear others can potentially help a particular individual and human being play a constructive role in the conflict resolution. It is also important to focus on a particular conflict only before getting into any other conflict or controversy. It means that the conflict resolution has to go on gradually and sequentially as compared to taking on a multitasking approach. The seeking of mutually agreed approach has to be floated by the affected parties, and individuals within a conflict ended situation. This can ultimately help the individuals encountered with a particular conflict find out an appropriate and agreeable conflict resolution scenario to get out of the challenging situation ultimate.

TECHNIQUE 31: TRACK EATING, SLEEPING, AND WORKING PATTERNS

Explore this question: What does eating, sleeping, and working patterns of a person tell us about his personality?

The eating, sleeping, and working patterns of a person tell a lot about his personality. Juliet Boghossian, a behavioral food expert, illustrates that food and eating habits can potentially help in the estimation and evaluation of a particular individual's personality. The different personalities can be associated with the different levels of the eating habits adopted by individuals. The food-specific habits of a particular individual can help in the exploration and evolution of the different facets and the personality-oriented characteristics of a particular individual. The behavioral tendencies related to the food-specific habits and eating of an individual can reflect a particular personality type acquired by that particular individual.

1.   The slow eaters usually like to be the people who want to remain in control, and they like to appreciate their life-oriented activities. There is a possibility that some of the people with slow eating abilities tend to feel pressurized as compared to the cutting speed of the other people around. They are capable of enjoying their food more as compared to the other types of eaters.

2.   The fast eaters may be potentially the people who earn more ambitious and only oriented within their lives. They usually try to catch up with different things within a specified range of the time which clearly indicates their ambitiousness to achieve certain targets.

3.   The isolationist and picky people, with respect to their eating habits, may be completely different in their personalities as they tend to lead more sequential actual lives. They usually tend to come out with different sorts of personality-oriented characteristics and lifestyle as compared to the other types of people with different eating habits.

The personality analysis, in the light of the eating habits, can be further integrated and connected with the sleeping as well as the word printed approach adopted by the individuals in their real life. The bottom line can be to look at the possibility related to the sleeping as well as the eating habits of an individual with the acceleration of certain characteristics of its personality. The comprehensive and in-depth analysis in the eating, as well as sleeping, behavior of individuals can help in the exploration of certain personality-oriented dynamics and the behaviors which they are more likely to exhibit in their real lives.

TECHNIQUE 32: DETECT AND EXAMINE WAYS OF EXPRESSING INNER TURMOIL AND PROFOUND THINKING

What is Inner Turmoil?

It's an emotional condition when a person is bound in self fears, hate, disgust, etc. It is the state in which a person is stressed out and self-pity himself. He feels agitated and confused. He starts self-torturing himself. No one gets into this depressing situation by choice, but some external factor makes the brain to behave like that.

Types of Inner Turmoil

There are certain types of turmoil's happens due to some specific situation.

1) Principled turmoil

2) Religious turmoil

3) Breakup turmoil

4) Low self-esteem turmoil

The Correlation between Internal and External

Turmoil

Internal turmoil is the conflict going on inside an individual. It's a fight between the inner emotions of the person and the external turmoil of the other persons or objects which creates panic and conflicts. They both can be interlinked because, most of the time, internal turmoil takes place due to the external turmoil. The major difference between the two is that inner turmoil cannot be seen, but the external turmoil is clearly visible if observed carefully.

How People Express Inner Turmoil

When it comes to getting rid of the internal turmoil or express their profound thinking, people adopt various ways in order to help get away with conflicting emotions running inside their minds. It's difficult to get out of your profound thinking, but it is only possible when the specific individual truly wants to come out from the traumatized state. There are numerous ways, but some are mentioned below:

By Talking

Talking to someone you are emotionally attached to will help you to get rid of that inner turmoil faster than you can imagine. Stress levels decrease when you share your emotions and know that the person you are conveying your emotions understands and feels your emotions well. And eventually, the words of comfort from that particular person gives a feeling of contentment.

By Being Creative

Rather than talking and sharing their emotions with someone, most people with inner turmoil opt for being creative. It can be anything like making paintings, creating artifacts, writing a good poem, etc. All these creative activities help a person with a turbulent mental state to feel better and relaxed. It acts as a catharsis for them.

By Exercising

It is rare, but there are people who take out themselves from inner turmoil by exercising. It can be jogging, weight training, Zumba, or any physical activity that can take them out from their mental stress in a manner that they feel lighter both physically and mentally.

By Watching Comedy Theatre

When getting out of inner turmoil, people also prefer to attend a good theatre program. Mostly, they opt for a comedy movie just to give themselves a good laugh and positivity.

By Relaxing with Animals and Nature

Animals can also act as your anti-depressant. Yes, it's true; some people find peace in nature and animals. They prefer to go into someplace nearer to nature or spend some time with their pets to bring back their minds on track.

By Sleeping

There is this strange habit in some people which, for them, sleep acts as a delete button. They put everything on a back burner and grab some hours of deep sleep to relax and refresh. When they wake up again, they often have already forgotten or eliminated the disturbing thoughts from their minds. Long and comfortable sleep makes them feel light-headed and full of regained energy for the day ahead.

❖ Bonus Question to Explore:

What do time management, future planning, goals, and leisure activities of a person tells us about his personality?

The time management and future planning skills and associated behavior of a particular person clearly indicate that his personality gets influenced by these change agents and behavior patterns. To perform the adequate level of personality analysis, you must explore these sorts of customized questions and brainstorm investigative ideas to come up with suitable, complementary information about a person's personality traits. There are different personality types that can be classified on the basis of looking at the time management skills of a particular individual. For instance:

1. The Time Martyrs: An individual who is more inclined towards focusing on spending time on behalf of others as compared to managing the time for itself may belong to this category of the time management personality type

2. The Wild Procrastinators: The procrastination can be potentially perceived as the opposite of productivity. It clearly means that Wild Procrastinators are the individuals

who are not capable of managing the time in the best way to enhance the level of the productivity and his struggle to achieve their life specific objectives as a whole

3. The Underestimators: These are the people that are usually underestimating the worth of their time responding to a particular task or project-specific accomplishment. The mistake regarding the estimation of the right time to complete a particular task of a project result in a negative way for them.

4. The Do-It-Alls: These are the individuals who try to focus on managing their activities in accordance with time. They try to give out the maximum level of productivity in order to perform the maximum level of the work in a given time duration.

5. The Commitment-Phobes: The free-spirited individuals usually focus on the level of the commitment more than the content of the constructive part of a particular project or task assigned to them. It means that in these personality types, you will be focused on the utilization of

the time in accordance with their particular moods.

Similarly, the leisure activities of a person also help in the identification of its particular personality. The hobbies and leisure activities can be combined with the time management and the futuristic planning-oriented abilities of individuals in order to find out the personality type precisely. The Do-It-Alls type personality may be considered as one of the best personality type looking at time management skills and the future planning abilities of the individuals. This type of personality can provide a particular individual with an ability to become more productive and objective with respect to the achievement of adequate objectives set within its lifestyle. There are still some of the characteristics associated with this particular most productive type of human personality responding to time management skills as it is not possible for a person to become 100% productive all the time. There should be a work-life balance in order to provide the individual with an ability to accomplish its tasks precisely and accurately.

CHAPTER 10

EMOTIONAL INTELLIGENCE AND PERSONALITY ANALYSIS

S ometimes lack of emotional IQ, simply known as EQ, also creates complications for efficient communication. An emotionally immature person will not be able to communicate well the way a person who is emotionally mature enough can do. An emotionally intelligent person can handle the situations calmly and peacefully.

TECHNIQUE 33

L ook into yourself, track your personality traits. Understand empathy vs. sympathy.

Put yourself in other's shoes. See, are you emotionally intelligent?

Intelligence can be measured in quotients. Most of us are familiar with the word IQ, which is intelligence quotients, in which our ability to memorize and logical reasoning is checked and EQ is emotional quotients in which persons handling of emotions in adversity are observed. Emotional intelligence is to recognize and understand other people's emotion or to stay calm and think sensibly during a panic situation.

Traits of Emotional Intelligence

Mentioned below are some qualities of a person having high emotional intelligence quotient:

Sympathy + Empathy Combination

On top of the list is the trait which shows kindness towards others. One with the kind heart and bright soul can think about others, and sometimes, even put himself in others' place as well in order to realize his state of mind. Generally, a person with good EQ thinks more about others than himself. A more detailed debate on sympathy vs. empathy will be discussed separately.

Self-Recognition

If a person understands himself well, he will be able to perform his responsibilities in a better way than the person who still doesn't realize his actual worth. It is necessary to keep analyzing yourself to improve and enhance yourself for a better life ahead.

Inquisitive Nature & Investigative Mind

An inquisitive person gets success easily because of his passion and curiosity to learn and grow. He observes his surroundings works with the curious mind thus gets what he wants in a minimum amount of time.

The most emotionally intelligent people are those who

work with an investigative mind. They always keep analyzing the information which comes in their path. They try to keep moving their mind in a manner to observe their habits and try to improve them in an efficient way.

Self Belief

You can't do anything if you don't believe in yourself. It's about self- control. Controlling your emotions is working with peace of mind. Once you start believing that everything happens for a reason, things get easy for survival. Hard work and a positive attitude are the key factors of a person's success. Doing meditation also makes your belief in yourself without any doubts.

Control on Desires

It's the best characteristic of an emotionally intelligent person that he doesn't get confused with the needs and wants. He stays focused and prefers to fulfill the needs first rather than the desires. It helps him set his priorities, thus making him focus on the actual goals of life.

Dedication

A true element present in an emotionally intelligent person is the dedication and his passion for his work, relations, and goals. He gives his best to get the maximum out of his efforts. Without dedication, no one can achieve the desired results.

Positive Approach

If an individual wants a steady success in life, then he must have to be optimistic about the things around him. He should build a positive attitude around himself so that no external element can destroy his focus.

Versatility & Adaptability

An emotionally intelligent person believes in versatility. He knows when to stop and when to indulge in some particular work or relation. He believes in adapting to situations in a positive manner and try to behave accordingly. He knows that adaptability is the quality which makes not only his life comfortable but others' too.

Empathy vs. Sympathy

Do you want satisfying and deep relations? You have to

understand the difference between empathy and sympathy.

❖ **Empathy:** It is an ability to understand the feelings of other people. Remember, empathy can fuel connections.

❖ **Sympathy:** It allows you to become a part of other's feelings. To drive connections, humans need compassion.

These are confusing terms in English, and people often use them interchangeably, as synonyms. Remember, these are related, but different words. Here is a brief explanation to understand the meaning and use of these words.

Sympathy (Seeing & Feeling)

Sympathy means concern or displaying caring emotions for someone. These emotions often come along with a wish to see him/her happy. It implies a sense of sharing similarities with profound engagement. Under this shared feeling, you can feel compassion, pity, or sorrow for others.

For instance, if your friend loses her father or any other loved one, you will feel sympathy for him/her and their family. In this situation, people can express this feeling with sadness. It can be difficult to feel empathy for this loss without having the same experience in your life.

Greeting cards with flowers for mourning families are sympathy cards. It means you have harmony with sufferers. Remember, feelings of sympathy for an organization are support, loyalty, and approval.

Empathy (Feeling & Understanding)

You can share and recognize the emotions of other people or even a fictional character. Empathy is an emotion that is stronger than sympathy. If you can put yourself in the same situation to understand the intensity of sadness or happiness of another person, it is empathy.

For instance, you are the kind of person who can't understand the feelings of another person unless you imagine yourself in his place. You have empathy if you can put yourself in a similar situation and perceive the feelings of another individual. Unfortunately, people often confuse empathy with compassion, sympathy, or pity.

If you are feeling uncomfortable seeing someone in a distressing or depressing situation, you are feeling pity. This emotion is less engaging than compassion, sympathy, or empathy. Empathy allows you to open up your senses and let the situation affect you in a way that you feel yourself responding to the call of emotions. It is challenging to feel empathetic without facing a similar situation in your life.

Right Time to Use the Term "Empathy"

Empathy allows you to identify and understand the feelings or situations of others. For instance, you can follow the condition of a homeless family because a cyclone once demolished your house. If you can put yourself in another's situation, the word empathy is right for you. Empathy is a noun, and for the very first time, it was used in 1895. This tells us that people started becoming emotionally intelligent back then.

Right Time to Use the Term "Sympathy"

Sympathy (again a noun) was used for the very first time in the 1500s. If you have feelings of pity or grief, you are showing solidarity. For instance, you can show sympathy to a grieving mother because, even though you have not experienced this situation yourself, you have a sensitive personality that lets you feel for others. Your personality traits include feelings such as kindness, generosity, care, and compassion.

Empathy means you are identifying another person's sorrow as your own. Therefore, you will be willing to walk the extra mile to support and protect that person as if you were doing that for yourself in a similar situation. Putting yourself in someone else's shoes will not only make you feel bad about a grieving person but make you want to make some positive changes as well to improve his situation. Suppose, you are looking at your friend while he tells you his emotional experience, a painful tale of past grievances. You are analyzing his expressions and sub-textual emotions while he speaks, and you notice his eyes well up. If you are an emotionally intelligent person having a high EQ rate, you would feel for his sorrow and the extent of his grief almost instantly. Maybe you would not even have to go as far as processing each word of his narrative to reach on a conclusion that he seeks support and empathy. Just looking at his tearful eyes, you may as well feel your eyes becoming teary.

Sometimes, sympathizing and saying sorry is not enough. Sometimes, a person does not just need a shoulder to cry on, and a pat on the back as consolation that everything would be fine. Sometimes, they just want you to cry with them instead of wiping their tears. Sometimes, you just need to let the flood gates open and get rid of all the accumulated debris and emotional baggage in order to feel lighthearted.

CONCLUSION

T hank you for making it through to the end of How to Analyze People and Understand the Human Mind. Let's hope it was informative and able to provide you with all of the tools you need to achieve your goals whatever they may be.

The next step is to transition from the book-practice to real-life practicum. The experiences are what make us into what we are today. After reading about the human personality analysis and people-reading with speed and quality methods, you are better equipped with the tools and techniques necessary to understand people and interact with them effectively. This is your chance to go out there and start proving your worth by not only differentiating your friends from your foes but also by turning the threat of failure into an opportunity for success. No longer should you fumble around with words to say in front of a stranger, or let misunderstandings ruin your relationships. Don't let people or environmental factors get the best of your efforts and well-intendedness nor let your misguided observation or judgmental views get the best of the good wishes of people around you. Look into their personality, try to understand their behavior, explore the possibilities, and analyze their intentions. This will help you in not only sustaining the old relationships along with building the new ones but also let you get successful by remaining one step ahead of your opponents.

Although we admit that the subject of human behavioral psychology is every vast, no way can it be summed up on a limited range of pages. However, we did try our best to accumulate the most sought after and relevant techniques that are easy to understand and focus more on action than mere wordiness so that they can be learned and implemented right away.

Finally, if you found this book useful in any way, a review on Amazon is always appreciated!

COGNITIVE BEHAVIORAL THERAPY MADE SIMPLE

Stop negative thinking and overcome anxiety and depression with CBT techniques for retraining your brain.

Peter Rajon

This eBook, Book is provided with the sole purpose of providing relevant information on a specific topic for which every reasonable effort has been made to ensure that it is both accurate and reasonable. Nevertheless, by purchasing this eBook, you consent to the fact that the author, as well as the publisher, are in no way experts on the topics contained herein, regardless of any claims as such that may be made within. As such, any suggestions or recommendations that are made within are done so purely for entertainment value. It is recommended that you always consult a professional prior to undertaking any of the advice or techniques discussed within.

This is a legally binding declaration that is considered both valid and fair by both the Committee of Publishers Association and the American Bar Association and should be considered as legally binding within the United States.

The reproduction, transmission, and duplication of any of the content found herein, including any specific or extended information will be done as an illegal act regardless of the end form the information ultimately takes. This includes copied versions of the work, both physical, digital, and audio unless the express consent of the Publisher is provided beforehand. Any additional rights reserved.

Furthermore, the information that can be found within the pages described forthwith shall be considered both accurate and truthful when it comes to the recounting of facts. As such, any use, correct or incorrect, of the provided information will render the Publisher free of responsibility as to the actions taken outside of their direct purview. Regardless, there are zero scenarios where the original author or the Publisher can be deemed liable in any fashion for any damages or hardships that may result from any of the information discussed herein.

The book COGNITIVE BEHAVIORAL THERAPY MADE SIMPLE: Stop negative thinking and overcome anxiety and depression with CBT techniques for retraining your brain., is reprinted by permission

INTRODUCTION

A nxiety is the persistent worry and fear that shows up in day-to-day living and makes life harder for the victim. A person with an anxiety disorder is usually affected by things that don't affect well-adjusted people with stable emotions. For most sufferers, the main reason behind their anxiety is cognitive distortions. In other words, their perception of their reality is flawed. As a result, they develop various self-inhibiting habits that ultimately make their condition even worse. Researchers have found that when a person is struggling with anxiety, there's a high likelihood that they are battling other forms of mental illness, especially depression.

But thanks to heaven, anxiety is not like some other nasty viral illnesses that have no cure yet. There are several treatment methods for anxiety and other mental illnesses. Most of these treatment methods have attracted nothing but positive reviews. Cognitive Behavioral Therapy is one of the most popular treatment plans for anxiety and other mental illnesses. The beauty of this treatment plan is that it can be practiced both during the Cognitive Behavioral Therapy course and even after.

This book looks at several mental health issues, namely, anxiety, depression, insomnia, and stress, and it shows how one might use Cognitive Behavioral Therapy to overcome these conditions.

Part I

CHAPTER 1

INTRODUCTION TO CBT

Y ou may have heard about Cognitive Behavioral Therapy, the treatment plan that is helping people overcome various mental illnesses. This treatment method has been so successful around the world, and more people are turning to it. If you have been considering to pursue this treatment, it is essential first to understand what you are getting into.

What is CBT?

Cognitive Behavioral Therapy is a type of psychotherapy. It is founded on the perception that most mental illnesses come about as a result of cognitive distortions. Thus, by pointing out these cognitive distortions and adopting helpful beliefs, the patient can overcome their mental illness. Unlike medicine, where it's just about swallowing pills and expecting results, Cognitive Behavioral Therapy requires the full participation of both the patient and the practitioner. Cognitive Behavioral Therapy involves various steps and procedures that must be followed over the course of time. Strict adherence to these steps and procedures always gives positive results. Most Cognitive Behavioral Therapy techniques can be practiced in day-to-day life, which means there is no limit to your improvement. Cognitive Behavioral Therapy takes on a holistic healing philosophy, and what's more, you get to understand how your brain perceives various things and people. In other words, Cognitive Behavioral Therapy helps you increase your self-awareness.

Did you know the number one cause of marital problems is poor communication? And when we talk about poor communication, we don't mean to say that partners have refused to speak to each other. They are talking to each other. But the problem is that each one of them gets a different message rather than what is intended. There are very many psychological factors that stop partners from understanding each other clearly. The importance of Cognitive Behavioral Therapy is that it draws attention to some of these factors that ultimately sabotage a relationship.

Cognitive Behavioral Therapy helps treat various conditions such as phobias, anxiety, major depressive disorder, dissociative disorder, personality disorders, self-esteem, and self-image issues. Cognitive Behavioral Therapy helps the patient understand most of their thought processes and see the connection between how they think and how they act. Since this treatment plan came into being, a lot of studies have been made to see its effectiveness, and so far, this treatment plan has been found to be extremely useful. Cognitive Behavioral Therapy posts even better results than people who are on medication.

Is CBT for me?

Most people find themselves wondering whether

Cognitive Behavioral Therapy is for them. But you have to understand that just because this treatment plan has been shown to work exceptionally well, the patient won't have to put any effort. In actual fact, the success of Cognitive Behavioral Therapy depends on the patient's effort. Thus, before you decide to follow this treatment plan, you must be ready to commit to the procedures, else you may end up wasting both your time and money.

What takes place during Cognitive Behavioral Therapy sessions & how long does it last?

At the start, the practitioner will find a way of ensuring that you both connect. Most practitioners have worked on their personalities, and they know how to handle different kinds of people. So, it is not uncommon for a practitioner to want to know about their patient's background. This helps them understand their patients even more. The practitioner opens up about the realities of Cognitive Behavioral Therapy. The patient needs to be aware of the various struggles that they will run into.

The practitioner gets to ask about the problem that is

dogging their patients. And the patient must try to be as forthcoming as possible. Some people are tempted to hold back parts that they feel ashamed of, but this is not a smart move; you must let it all out. Then the practitioner offers the patient various steps and procedures that are aimed at identifying your cognitive distortions. The patient must adhere to these steps and procedures.

The amount of time it takes to achieve positive results with Cognitive Behavioral Therapy is dependent on the efforts of both the practitioner and the patient, and also the kind of problem being dealt with. But in a general sense, Cognitive Behavioral Therapy is more time-efficient than various other treatment methods. For instance, if you swallowed pills to become euphoric and numb yourself from feelings of low self-esteem, you might have to swallow those pills forever. But when it comes to Cognitive Behavioral Therapy, it is a matter of establishing the root cause of your self-esteem issues, and then developing new positive beliefs about yourself, and applying these principles into your daily life, and the self-esteem issue is gone.

Using Cognitive Behavioral Therapy techniques beyond the course

One of the benefits of Cognitive Behavioral Therapy is the fact that you can continue practicing these steps way after your course. A skilled practitioner will give you knowledge. And this knowledge is what keeps you going. You will find that various steps won't require any spending of money. It is up to you to just find the time. So, by incorporating these Cognitive Behavioral Therapy steps into your life, you solidify the effectiveness of this treatment plan. There are various resources, such as books, magazines, and online portals, to help you along the way.

Does science support CBT? Is it successful?

Some people might want to find out whether Cognitive Behavioral Therapy is backed by science. This is a very legitimate concern, considering that most people are a victim to pseudo-scientific disciplines. Scientists have analyzed the effectiveness of Cognitive Behavioral Therapy. They have studied how patients that go through the entire course of Cognitive Behavioral Therapy fare against similar patients who have undergone other forms of treatment. They found out that patients who have undergone Cognitive Behavioral Therapy tend to recover fully simply because the results are lasting. But for patients who, e.g., Take medicine, they might relapse into their previous mental state, which is basically back to step one.

During a CBT course, these are some of the things that you will learn:

•   Identify problems more clearly: CBT helps you have a clearer picture of what's behind your problems. Talk therapy is designed to get to the root of the problem.

•   Develop an awareness of automatic thoughts: your automatic thoughts are responsible for your negative behaviors and actions. CBT helps you understand your automatic thoughts when they come up.

•   Challenge underlying assumptions that may be wrong: negative thoughts and twisted perceptions can stem from inaccurate presumptions. CBT helps you uncover the inaccurate assumptions you may hold.

•   Distinguish between facts and irrational thoughts: some complications come about as a result of holding onto irrational thoughts for the longest time. CBT helps you identify what's factual and get rid of the irrational beliefs that have held you as a hostage as well as given you bad traits.

• Understand how past experiences can affect present experiences: for most people who struggle with mental health issues, particularly depression, their past is to blame. Something traumatic went down in the past that triggered their depression. CBT helps them identify what these past problems are and get over them. The healing process starts once they have overcome their terrible past experiences.

• Stop fearing the worst: most people develop mental illnesses that are anchored on their fear for the worst. For instance, if you tend to worry about what would happen if you are alone in a dark room, CBT helps you understand that nothing would happen at all, and your fear is imagined.

• See a situation from a different perspective: one of the problems that people have when it comes to mental illnesses is an inability to have various aspects to the same thing. Most negative thought patterns can be overcome when you start perceiving life from more than one angle. It stimulates your creativity and helps you overcome your present challenge.

• Better understand other peoples' actions and

motivations: we don't live in a vacuum. We live in a space inhabited by other people. Their efforts are bound to influence our lives, whether we like it or not. Thus, we had better understand other peoples' actions and motivations. If we know what motivates them, we are in a better position to take self-preserving decisions and not falling prey to them.

• Develop a more positive way of thinking and seeing situations: the value of keeping a positive mind in the face of trouble cannot be overstated. It makes all the difference. CBT helps people develop a positive mindset and face their challenges without falling into vices and other harmful habits.

• Become more aware of their mood: if you are battling mental illnesses, you are likely to experience terrible feelings for most of the time. CBT helps you uncover the relationship between your thoughts, actions, and beliefs. If you engage in harmful activities, you have a high likelihood of experiencing low moods.

• Establish attainable goals: at the end of the day, everyone wants to see their dreams come true. The problem is that some of these dreams are more life delusions. If you set a goal that has no chance of ever coming to life, you set yourself up for failure. CBT helps you stay grounded and have the presence of mind required to craft attainable goals.

• Avoid generalizations and all-or-nothing thinking: we shouldn't think in absolute terms. There are certainly gray areas. By embracing CBT, we get to understand the value of paying attention to the gray areas instead of an all-or-nothing mindset.

• Stop blaming yourself: some people shift blame to themselves for things that were totally beyond their control. This makes it hard for them to overcome the problem. Through CBT, they can understand the value of objectivity and not just burdening themselves with unwarranted blame.

• Focus on the present: CBT might help you understand your past and prepare for the future, but the main emphasis is the present. CBT techniques are aimed at working with whatever that's going on at present. Thus, CBT provides a very accurate remedy for your troubles.

• Face your fears: if you have been battling fears, you might have developed several negative thinking patterns, and twisted perception of reality, that have no doubt gifted you a mental illness such as paranoia or phobias. CBT helps you face your fears and emerge triumphantly.

How CBT works

Your actions are influenced by your thoughts, feelings, and physical sensations. When you give room to negative thoughts, you end up trapped in a cycle of degenerative behaviors and actions. CBT helps you break down a problem into small bits so that you can deal with it far easier. It allows you to change these negative patterns to improve how you feel. Unlike other treatment models that focus on past issues, CBT focuses on what's troubling you at present, promoting appropriate thoughts, behaviors, and habits.

Problems are broken down into five main groups:

- Physical feelings
- Situations
- Actions
- Thoughts
- Emotions

These five areas are interconnected. For instance, your thoughts about a specific situation might affect your feelings, as well as the response that you are going to give. CBT is different than other psychotherapies in the following aspects:

• It's pragmatic: specific problems are identified, and work begins in solving them.

• Highly structured: the therapist and the patient identify specific challenges and set goals as a way of finding a solution.

• Focused on the present: CBT focuses on what your thoughts, emotions, and habits are like at present as opposed to focusing on your past.

• Collaborative: the success of this talking therapy is, in a significant sense, dependent upon the relationship between the therapist and the patient. The two must work together to find a lasting solution.

There are convenient and inconvenient ways of approaching a problem, depending on your thought system. For example, if your marriage partner deserts you and files for divorce, you might think that you are a failure, and consider yourself unworthy of finding love again. This line of thought could make you hopeless and lonely, turning you into a hermit that detests people and trapped in a vicious cycle of negativity, you feel bad about yourself and self-sabotage against ever being in a meaningful relationship.

On the other side, you could make peace with the fact that divorce is not the end of your love life. Many people get past it and live to their full potential. Developing optimism for the future will influence your habits and actions. You will start going out more, taking up different activities, and eventually, you'll run into someone that your heart beats for.

The above example is a perfect illustration of how your thoughts, feelings, and physical sensations can hold you in a cycle of negativity, and even create new situations that worsen how you feel about yourself. It shows that if you want to turn your life around, you must begin by exploring your mental constitution, and commit to altering your thoughts and feelings.

CBT seeks to put an end to such negative cycles, by exposing the associated thoughts and emotions and empowering you to turn your life around. CBT techniques are designed in such a manner that after a certain point, you don't need a therapist to break the negative cycles, but just your dedication.

CBT Sessions

You can carry out CBT sessions as an individual or a group with a therapist, but if you have some substantial experience, you might not even need a therapist. If you have CBT as an individual or as a group, you'll generally meet with the therapist five to twenty times for weekly or fortnightly sessions, with each session taking about 30 – 60 minutes. The sessions may take place anywhere both of you are comfortable: clinic, outdoor, home.

Cognitive Behavioral Therapy Techniques

These are some of the techniques in CBT used to modify a person's behavioral patterns:

• Cognitive rehearsal: the patient starts by calling to mind their traumatic events, and with the help of a therapist, they work toward a solution. The patient has to instill positive thoughts in their mind to strengthen their positive attitude and encourage the development of positive traits. The part about rehearsing positive thoughts requires a bit of imagination.

• Validity testing: in this technique, the therapist seeks to test whether the patient's beliefs are valid or invalid. The patient can bring up objective evidence to defend their feelings, but if their argument is weak, then the inaccuracy of their belief is exposed, and they are encouraged to create accurate beliefs.

• Writing a journal: a patient takes upon themselves to note down the happenings of their life to trace maladaptive behaviors. The patient notes down all the critical things taking place in their life, at the emotional, mental, and physical plane, and together with the therapist, they may review these events to find out the interconnectedness between these areas.

• Guided discovery: patients may exhibit negative tendencies when they have a flawed perception of reality. But a therapist would assist them in comprehending their cognitive distortions. Patients become more aware of how they process information. In the end, patients can adopt an accurate perception of reality, and it helps them process information accurately.

• Modeling: it is one of the most critical techniques in straightening out a patient. A therapist may perform role-playing exercises from which the patient may draw inspiration to change their behavior. It helps the patient understand the perfect ways of response to various scenarios.

• Homework: in this technique, the patient is asked to perform various tasks to draw lessons that will impact their mindset and help them modify their behaviors. Some of the tasks include reviewing audiotapes, taking notes, and reading articles.

• Systematic positive reinforcement: in this technique, a patient is encouraged to bring out more of their positive traits. It's far easier to modify a person's behaviors when their positive characteristics are dominant. Thus, a therapist would identify a patient's positive traits, and then reward the patient for every time their positive habits or attitudes are applied.

CHAPTER 2

REASONS WHY CBT IS GROWING IN POPULARITY

A t any given time, the average person is battling a set of problems that invariably have a mental origin. This is simply because our thoughts heavily regulate our actions and behaviors. For instance, let's say you step out of your house, and while you're walking in the street, you catch a reflection of yourself and decide that you look awful. That very thought seeds doubt in your mind and lowers your self-esteem and perhaps makes you irritable for the rest of the day. But if you had the understanding of your psychology, you might not have gone down that path. As a treatment method, Cognitive Behavioral Therapy is enjoying a lot of success in the world, thanks to its ability to overcome not only the negative symptoms of an ailment but also increase the patient's self-awareness.

The following are some of the reasons why Cognitive Behavioral Therapy has become such a success all over the world:

- **Proven track record**

At the end of the day, success is a numbers game. It would be a bit illogical to claim that Cognitive Behavioral Therapy is the best treatment method without having the numbers to back up that claim. But then, Cognitive Behavioral Therapy has been shown to treat various illnesses, among them major depressive disorder, panic attacks, various anxiety disorders, drug abuse, eating disorders, insomnia, trauma, and phobias. Patients who underwent Cognitive Behavioral Therapy have been shown to achieve lasting results, which makes undergoing the treatment worthwhile.

- **It does not interrupt your life**

Perhaps one of the biggest reasons why we fail to seek medical help is the fear that it will disrupt our day-to-day lives, and this fear is logical considering that life is about chasing money, and not most of us have been successful enough to set passive income streams. So, we are always looking for a solution that won't have us stay away from work. Think about someone battling major depressive disorder and decides to take medication. Now upon swallowing the heavy medication, they obviously won't go on with their lives, but they have to stay indoors to recover. Being away from work for an extended period can have serious implications.

But then here comes a form of treatment that won't necessarily have you stay away from work. It involves various procedures that you can follow with ease and get on to other work. The patient might take these Cognitive Behavioral Therapy sessions at the time that they consider convenient. In that way, their lives are virtually unaffected.

- **It's inexpensive**

Another reason why Cognitive Behavioral Therapy has found enormous success across the world is down to the fact that seeking this treatment plan won't hurt your pockets. When a patient decides to use medication to treat their mental illness, it usually takes a long time before positive results can be seen. But then these drugs don't come cheap. The pharmaceutical companies are looking to make a significant profit. In the long run, the patient ends up spending a ton of money on drugs. But the patient who pursues Cognitive Behavioral Therapy techniques ends up spending considerably less.

- It takes a short amount of time

You cannot say how long a Cognitive Behavioral Therapy course for a particular patient will last. This is because the length of a CBT course is affected by various factors, including finances, effort, and convenience. But in some cases, patients have been reported to witness positive results within as short a time as six weeks. This is an incredible advantage considering that some other treatment methods may run into months or even years. CBT takes less time to overcome mental illness, but the best part about it is that the results are permanent, which cannot be said of various other treatment methods.

- ### It's empowering

One of the significant benefits of a Cognitive Behavioral Therapy course besides healing is that it empowers the patient. For one, the patient has a deeper understanding of how their actions, words, and mindset correlates with their thoughts. You find that most patients are previously unaware of this fact. A Cognitive Behavioral Therapy course helps the patient take the wheel when it comes to their mental health. When all the procedures are laid bare, it is for the patient to follow these procedures, implement them in their lives, so that the results can be even better. But this does not mean that they won't need therapy anymore, only that it will empower them.

- ### It's a team effort

When a person is battling some form of mental illness, they usually have a terrible attitude, which is a significant disadvantage, considering that they have no motivation. For instance, if a mentally ill person visits a physician and ends up hooked medication, it is upon him to take the dosage appropriately, without anyone caring for his progress. But when you look at a Cognitive Behavioral Therapy course, the skilled practitioner is always going to be there to encourage the patient to follow through with all the procedures. This encouragement plays a critical role in the overall success of the treatment method.

- **It's simplified**

In a Cognitive Behavioral Therapy course, everything is not thrown at once at the patient. The course is designed in ascending order of difficulty. The early stages comprise of simple exercises that will help the patient develop a great mindset. But as the course advances, they are introduced into more challenging procedures, but then it becomes much easier to overcome these procedures because they have the right mindset.

- **It's safe**

One of the ugly sides to medication is the side effects. Most drugs that are intended to eliminate anxiety come with a long list of side effects, including poor vision, diarrhea, dizziness, pain, exhaustion, migraines, and dry mouth. Assuming that the medicine works to eliminate the symptoms of the mental illness the patient was struggling with, that's good enough, but then the side effects make it worse. When it comes to a Cognitive Behavioral Therapy course, there are no side effects, but more importantly, the results of a Cognitive Behavioral Therapy course are permanent.

- **Therapists are nice**

Some people think that the health industry attracts a lot of psychopaths. They might have reached this conclusion after being mistreated by a nurse, a pharmacist, or even a doctor. Considering the demands of most medical jobs, the professionals can be easily stressed, and start taking it out on innocent people; not that it's intentional. But then you cross over to Cognitive Behavioral Therapy and find that the therapists are friendly. They have been trained on how to handle all types of personalities. And so, it doesn't matter how off-the-charts your character might appear to be, but your therapist will connect with you.

Part II

CHAPTER 3

UNDERSTANDING ANXIETY

A nxiety is a perfectly normal biological response. It is a natural force that heightens our self-preservation in dangerous circumstances. So, if you find yourself having to walk to a member of the opposite sex and pour out your heart's content, it's perfectly normal to be anxious. It's perfectly normal to experience anxiety from time to time. But then, if you find yourself being anxious for most of the day so that your excessive anxiety interferes with your day-to-day living, you're most definitely struggling with an anxiety disorder.

But then you're not alone. Research says that approximately 40 million Americans struggle with an anxiety disorder every year, which means the real figure could be far higher, considering that public awareness of mental illness is pretty minimal.

Anxiety disorders are serious health issues. They deserve as much attention as physical health disorders. An anxiety disorder may not be as conspicuous to a third party as a physical illness, but then the sufferer experiences the problematic symptoms.

Generalized anxiety disorder

Someone who suffers from generalized anxiety disorder tends to struggle with an impulsive anxiety streak. And most of their anxiety attacks arise from flimsy reasons. Someone who's struggling with generalized anxiety disorder cannot function normally in society. In a social setting, such a person easily comes across as a weirdo because of their inability to read social cues. People may react by treating them with suspicion or barring them from their circles.

People struggling with a generalized anxiety disorder may experience the symptoms for up to six months, and this anxiety is attributed to virtually all areas of their life such as health, work, relationships, school, and even hobbies.

Considering that generalized anxiety disorder stops one from leading a healthy existence, it is only fair that the victim concentrates on overcoming his plight. There are various treatment avenues that the victim might consider, but on the whole, Cognitive Behavioral Therapy is the most effective.

People who struggle with generalized anxiety disorder have a hard time fitting in society. If the problem is not resolved, they may actually never fit in. And considering that some of our essential needs require others to be fulfilled, it is incredibly vital to overcoming this condition.

Panic disorder

Let's say you were lying in your bed at night when suddenly the lights went off. What followed was an eerie silence in your apartment, and although you were alert, nothing really worried you. But then you made out the sound of oncoming footsteps. Someone was at your door, knocking wildly, and before you could answer, they started to kick it down. It makes sense that in such a situation, you would panic. You would start sweating, trembling, your heart would race, and you would entertain thoughts of impending doom. But then this would be an appropriate response considering what you are facing. I mean, if someone is trying to kick your door down, obviously they're not bringing any significant news. But what if you experience the sweating and those feelings of impending doom throughout your day? Would that be normal? Hell no! But then that is the reality of someone who's struggling with panic disorder.

This condition causes people to experience unexpected panic attacks. The panic attacks are basically periods of intense fear that cause a person to shake, sweat, and even think that they are about to die. This type of fear accelerates way fast. And the triggers for this condition are not necessarily huge. But then that seemingly flimsy trigger evokes an intense dread in the victim's mind.

Someone who's suffering from panic attacks will keep worrying about when the next attack might happen, and then they will try their best to hold it off by avoiding scenarios, people, or things that they associate with panic.

Obsessive-Compulsive disorder

An obsessive-compulsive disorder is characterized by repetitive and unwanted thoughts that cause the victim to act compulsively. Someone with an obsessive-compulsive disorder cannot function normally in society. Their compulsive habits make them seem odd. They cannot perform unless they have answered to their compulsive urge. For instance, if you obsess about getting ill, you might develop a compulsive habit of washing hands. So, no matter what you touch, you must wash your hands. It could be something as innocent as placing your hands on a table, and then the obsessive thought clicks into being, "oh no! You've got to wash your hands now!" and you won't settle until you have washed your hands.

Let's say you have obsessive thoughts that are sexual in

nature. So, you keep playing out these scenarios of wild sex in your mind, and you have the urge to either have sex or watch pornography, and that urge doesn't go until you give in to your "thirst." Slowly, you find yourself stuck in this cycle.

Social Anxiety Disorder

People who struggle with social anxiety disorder have a strong aversion to social engagements. They will do their best to escape instances in which they have to socialize with anybody else. The thing about a social anxiety disorder is that the affected people resent it too. This means that in their hearts o hearts, the victim wants to be free enough to mingle with people, except they cannot help themselves but feel frightened about it. Social anxiety disorder usually comes about when a person thinks that they are incomplete in some way. For instance, if a young woman thinks herself ugly, she may develop an aversion to mingling with other people, for she figures that other people may laugh at her.

PTSD

Post-traumatic stress disorder is a pretty much common

mental illness. It usually fueled by past unresolved trauma. One category of Americans who are prone to PTSD is the military. After years of witnessing the ugly side of human beings, it can easily come back to haunt them. If one had been deployed to a war-torn country and engaged the local militia in gunfire, it doesn't take away the fact that they killed people, and in a battlefield, death comes in a most jarring manner. When a former military man gets away from the battlefield into some other field, they find out that they never really got over what they had seen, and it comes to them in the form of PTSD. These traumatic experiences are relived through vivid flashbacks, obsessive thoughts, visions, and even daydreams.

CHAPTER 4

SYMPTOMS OF ANXIETY

Excessive worrying

One of the common symptoms of an anxiety disorder is excessive worrying. This comes about as a result of thinking too hard on life, and as a result, getting hurt by things that don't hurt ordinary people. Many people have developed this habit of excessive worrying, and it stops them from leading a productive life. If you find yourself worrying excessively over seemingly little things, you might be battling an anxiety disorder. In order to realize that you have a problem that needs to be overcome, you have to increase your level of self-awareness and understand that your words and actions are indicative of a more significant problem.

- **Feeling agitated**

Another common sign that one is battling anxiety disorder is a tendency to be agitated. When a person develops anxiety, their body is literally put on the fight or flight mode, and as a result, their brain nourishes their muscles with excessive blood, so as to prepare that person for whatever comes out, and as a result, the person becomes agitated. If you are usually a calm person, and you suddenly find yourself being super-agitated over stuff that people are doing or not doing, you might be struggling with an anxiety disorder. But then again, simply because you feel agitated doesn't mean that you automatically have an anxiety disorder. It makes sense first to understand your situation.

- **Restlessness**

This symptom is particularly real for children and young adults. In a study of young people who reported a struggle with anxiety, it was found that upwards of 70% of these kids were restless. Being restless refers to the constant urge to be on the move. A restless person cannot stay in one place. And this brings about confusion into their life. Restlessness tends to accelerate poor decision making as the victim doesn't have the patience to collect their thoughts together and make a decision that serves their interests. If you find yourself being restless, you might want to look keenly, whether you have an anxiety disorder.

- **Fatigue**

It is perfectly normal to experience fatigue after indulging in heavy work like moving house. But if you have a tendency to become fatigued after performing simple tasks or no tasks at all, that is deeply alarming. People who battle anxiety disorder keep on experiencing fatigue. This fatigue usually comes about as a result of the overthinking and restlessness that victims subject themselves to. Obviously, it becomes pretty hard to do anything productive when you are out of energy for most of your time. So, if you find yourself becoming exhausted for no reason, check to see that your anxiety is treated before it makes your life unbearable.

- **Lack of concentration**

In order to make a positive impact in your life, you have to put in some effort. Nothing worth achieving ever comes easy. It takes hard work. But in order to work hard, you must concentrate on your work. Most people who struggle with anxiety have a hard time concentrating on what they are doing. And this obviously affects the quality of their output. Lack of concentration is a big sign that your emotional and mental environment is in chaos, and unless you work on making your emotional world calm, you won't be able to focus on whatever you are doing.

- **Irritability**

People battling an anxiety disorder have a reputation for being nasty. People around them may put effort into being nice, but they get paid with even more nastiness. An irritable person walks around with a scowl, ready to get mad at anything or anyone that crosses his path, and for that reason, people shun him. And since human beings are mostly social animals, it becomes really terrible for them, as they cannot make sense of why nobody wants to be close to them. It cannot be easy to realize that you are an irritable person because you will always rationalize your actions. But to overcome irritability, you have first to address your anxiety disorder.

• Tense muscles

People who are battling anxiety disorders report having muscle pain. Anxiety puts your brain into an overactive state, and this condition is not very helpful to your body, as it strains the resources. Then you start to experience pain in certain areas of your body. The body is composed of many parts, and for it to run smoothly, every part must work efficiently. When your emotions or thoughts are supportive of anxiety, it brings about pain to specific muscles. One of the most effective ways of overcoming anxiety is through muscle relaxation therapy.

• Insomnia

One of the factors that help lead to a productive life is quality sleep. We should get at least seven hours of sleep every night. But then some people have trouble falling asleep. They may get into bed and fail to get even a wink of sleep for the better part of the night. The little sleep they get has its shortcomings. It causes them to achieve subpar results in whatever activity they engage in. Insomnia is one of the indications that a person is battling an anxiety disorder.

- **Too much sleep**

On the opposite end of insomnia, we have people who have trouble stepping out of bed. They want to jump into their bed and while the hours away. Of course, such people are scared of real-life and are trying to escape their challenges through sleep. But then one cannot run away from their life! Ultimately you reach a point where you have no option but to confront your reality. If you find yourself sleeping way more than it's necessary, you might be suffering from an anxiety disorder, and you are looking to run away from your reality.

- **Panicking**

Another clear sign that you are battling an anxiety disorder is a tendency to panic. And this feeling is usually triggered by flimsy reasons. It could be something as simple as watching a scary movie, but then it stimulates your hidden fears, and you find yourself panicking. In such instances, you might even think that your death is imminent, failing to recognize that the incident you just saw was fictional and that your fear is imagined really.

- **Avoiding people**

Another reliable indicator that you have an anxiety disorder is a tendency to run away from human interaction. You must first understand that human beings play a critical role in our wellbeing. To be truly happy, we must put other human beings into the equation, and it's because we need other people in order to fulfill our essential needs. When someone actively avoids engagement, that might be an indication that they have an anxiety disorder.

CHAPTER 5

CAUSES OF ANXIETY

I t's not enough to know that you are ailing from anxiety. It's just as important to understand how your anxiety came about. The following are some of the causes of stress.

• **Health issues**

You need to be in perfect health in order to lead a healthy life and achieve your important life goals. Without health, you are pretty much done for. Thus, when you develop a condition that is hugely detrimental to your physical health, you may find yourself developing anxiety. For instance, if you acquire an incurable disease, the idea that you won't overcome this disease may embitter your spirit and cause you to become anxious. It is important to remind yourself that you will overcome whatever physical ailment you find yourself struggling against in order not to develop negative thoughts that usually mature into anxiety.

- **Medication**

Some prescriptions and over-the-counter drugs can bring about anxiety. This is because the ingredients in these medicines might make you uneasy. If you fail to follow the instructions on proper consumption of medication, it can put you at risk of developing anxiety. If you have been put on heavy medication for a significantly large amount of time, you can quickly become overwhelmed from the constant consumption of medicine, and consequently, develop a poor self-image. It wouldn't be uncommon for you to think out loud; "what's wrong with me?" some of the medications that are notorious for causing anxiety include birth control pills and weight loss pills.

- **Caffeine**

Some people can't face their day without getting their glorious caffeine fix for the day. But this is the big question: is caffeine good for you? And the answer is: probably not! Research has found that being a heavy coffee drinker could put you at risk of developing anxiety. If you realize that you get anxious every time you drink coffee, you might want to get away from this habit, so that you may have a chance of improving your mental and emotional health. Many drinks make for great substitutes for coffee.

- **Skipping meals**

Some people might have read online that skipping meals will help them lose weight. Instead of going the long and hard route that involves watching what you eat and developing powerful habits, they simply starve themselves. But then starving yourself has several adverse health effects, and then the lost weight is usually water-weight, which means soon the kilos will spring back. But what's even worse is the fact that putting yourself in starvation mode can cause anxiety. If you're looking to lose weight, instead of skipping meals, just ensure that you watch your diet and engage in physical exercises.

• Negativity

Your mind plays a crucial role in how you act or talk. If you are full of positive energy, you find yourself making positive decisions, and if you are full of negative energy, you find yourself making bad decisions. One of the profound ways that negativity holds you down is by inviting anxiety into your life. If you are used to looking at yourself in a negative light, you will have only nasty things to say of yourself, and it will encourage you to have self-inhibiting tendencies. A negative mindset causes you to develop anxiety and ultimately stops you from reaching your important life goals.

• Financial challenges

It is near impossible to be happy when you are debt-laden. But then you don't need millions to be a happy person. If you lack the funds to cater for your primary and secondary needs, you can become somewhat frustrated, or even mad with your life. Financial challenges have pushed people into doing terrible things. If your finances are not in order, you can easily find yourself developing anxiety. The best way to ensure that you are not financially weak is to develop marketable skills, network with others, and expand your entrepreneurial spirit.

- **Social events**

Social engagements are another major cause of anxiety. Many people are uncomfortable with having to interact with strangers. It partly stems from a fear of judgment. If you're scared of meeting people, you tend to develop anxiety whenever you are in a social environment. If you're one of those people who are afraid of interacting with strangers, you might want to bring along a friend into social functions.

- **Conflict**

If you're used to having conflicts in your life, it not only increase stress, but it might also trigger an anxiety disorder. The brain has marked out conflicts as nasty experiences. So, your mind will always be looking for ways to get away from conflicts. Thus, you may find yourself getting affected by things that don't affect ordinary people. Let's say that one of your major trouble is handling a relationship. Maybe you read too much in your partner's words or actions, stoking your feelings. Your brain will make you alive to the events that precede scenarios that you consider disrespectful. In the long run, you are trapped in a negative and vicious cycle.

- **Weight loss supplements**

We live in an age where it's so easy to get fat. Our diets are poor. And our lifestyles are pretty much sedentary. It starts out slowly before you know it, you are on the overweight territory. The best way to stay in great shape and weight is through observing a great diet and working out. But who's got the time for that? Some quasi health-practitioners tell us that we can work our way around that by swallowing diet pills. For one, the advantages of these diet pills have been discredited, but then it seems that that pills can cause one to develop anxiety, it's a loss, either way, you look at it.

- **Excessive stress**

As long as you live on this planet, you will always have to deal with stress. But then you have to understand that some levels of stress are manageable while others are totally crippling. With manageable stress, you only need a good laugh, and you'll be over it, but when the stress becomes unmanageable, it spreads around all areas of your life, holding you captive. Psychologists believe that excessive stress is a major cause of anxiety. Circumstances that promote excessive stress depend from person to person, but some of the common areas include joblessness, death of a loved one, divorce, and chronic illness.

CHAPTER 6

RISK FACTORS FOR ANXIETY

R isk factors are merely the things that increase the likelihood of you getting a disease. When it comes to anxiety, various risk factors increase your likelihood of developing that condition. Although one might develop an anxiety disorder without any of these risk factors, their presence makes it more likely to develop the condition. The following are some of the risk factors for developing an anxiety disorder.

- **Sex**

Statistics show that women are much more likely to have an anxiety disorder than men. One of the main reasons why women have a higher rate of anxiety disorder is because of their willingness to visit a doctor, talk about their symptoms, and get a diagnosis. Women also have hormones that predispose them to anxiety disorders. Cultural expectation is another factor that puts women more at risk of developing an anxiety disorder than men. Women are obviously more concerned about what society thinks of them than men are. So, you'll find a woman stressing about things that don't affect the average man, which can push her into an anxiety disorder.

- **Family history**

An anxiety disorder can run in the family. Some so many families are known for particular health conditions. When it comes to anxiety, members of a family can be predisposed to the condition, particularly due to family dynamics. Some of these dynamics include abuse, violence, and over-protection. The family may have a way of doing things that predisposes them to an anxiety disorder. As more family members adopt the methods of their larger family, they find themselves at risk of developing this condition. It can be hard to overcome this challenge considering that our families mostly influence human behavior.

- **Genetics**

When you talk of anxiety running in the family, it is usually as a result of family members going about their lives in a way that encourages these anxiety disorders. But then an anxiety disorder can very well be ingrained in an individual's genetics. If someone is genetically predisposed to an anxiety disorder, they might pass down that condition to their offspring. In the case of genetic predisposition to an anxiety disorder, there's not much that can be done to overcome the condition, except learning the best coping skills.

- **Substance abuse**

When someone starts abusing drugs, they usually are trying to get away from their reality. They might be disillusioned with their life. They might be deeply disappointed about something. Or they may have no sense of direction. And these are not the right places to be as a human being. And so, they turn to drugs in an effort to numb their feelings. The thing about drugs is that they can make those horrible feelings go away, but only for a moment. Once the effects of the drug subside, the previous feelings come back with even higher intensity, commonly throwing the victim into episodes of anxiety.

- **Chronic illness**

When one is dealing with a disease that persists for months or even years, they are at risk of developing an anxiety disorder. Most chronic diseases come with a subset of nasty realities that make life tough. For instance, diabetes, a common chronic disease, makes it hard for the victim to lead a healthy life. They are restricted from specific diets that they probably once enjoyed. Also, their body seems to take a beating thanks to the heavy medication. All of these factors increase the likelihood of a person developing an anxiety disorder.

- **Ethnic factors**

Human beings are social animals. When one finds

themselves surrounded by people that they cannot relate with, it can cause them tremendous emotional pain that could ultimately trigger the development of anxiety. In the present age, there is a lot of migration from third world countries into first world countries. Most of these immigrants are at risk of developing anxiety disorders. This is because of; difficulties adjusting to a new culture, inferiority complex, isolation, lack of strong family ties, and facing hostility from the host.

• Depression

The funny thing about mental illness is that it shows up in a pair of conditions or more. You find that most people suffering from an anxiety disorder are also dealing with a major depressive disorder and maybe even other conditions. Depression is one of the most common forms of mental illness. It is characterized by long-running periods of feeling low and discouraged. Depressed people struggle with feelings of loss of hope. And this condition usually puts one at risk of developing an anxiety disorder.

• Trauma

A traumatic experience leaves the victim overwhelmed with feelings of pain and loss. It can be pretty hard to overcome a traumatic experience. For some people, they have to live with daily reminders of that traumatic experience, which is not a good thing. Now what usually happens is that this traumatic experience causes the victim to develop a warped perception of reality that predisposes them to mental illness, and specifically, an anxiety disorder. Most people who struggle with unresolved trauma not only find it hard to fit in society, but they also struggle with being productive.

• Social media

Human beings are collectively very innovative. One of the areas we have made tremendous advancement is in technology. We now have the internet, which has revolutionized the world, and the internet, as a resource, is arguably responsible for creating more wealth than any other resource in the planet's history. Thanks to the internet, we now have various social media platforms, and researchers have found that the average person is spending many hours on the social media platform. But then psychologists warn us that social media could predispose us to mental illnesses such as anxiety. When you have a habit of checking out your social media, you are basically trying to measure yourself against the world, and in most cases, you'll find yourself coming up short, which will ultimately make you feel bad.

- **Suicidal intent**

People who tend to inflict self-harm are at a greater risk of developing an anxiety disorder. Such people might have done things like cutting themselves, flinging themselves into a river, or even banging their heads against hard objects. Such behaviors are indicative of a profound loss of hope. For a person who is looking to end their life, nothing ever feels right, and this predisposes them towards developing a host of mental health issues.

CHAPTER 7

NEGATIVE EFFECTS OF ANXIETY ON PHYSICAL HEALTH

M ost people imagine that anxiety disorder only affects an individual's behavior. But there are also many effects of anxiety on physical health. Here are some of them.

- **Increased heartbeat**

You must remember that anxiety is a perfectly normal biological response. This response has helped us survive the threat of extinction. When we find ourselves in a situation that causes us to be anxious, our brain figures out that we need to either fight or flee and as a result, it causes our heart to beat more rapidly, thus sending blood to all the critical muscles to enable our fight or flee response. The problem with a racing heartbeat is that it brings about many other unfavorable conditions, for instance, confusion, dizziness, and feeling weak. It becomes so much harder to do the things that you are used to doing comfortably.

- **Shortness of breath**

Let's assume that you are deeply anxious about darkness. When your partner is around, you're not really that scared, but when they are gone, those haunting thoughts come back. So, one day, your partner travels away, and you are left alone in the house, which makes your sort of uneasy. At night you decide to sleep with the lights on because you're obviously scared of the dark. But before you fall asleep, there is a power outage. You start experiencing haunting feelings and thoughts. As your heartbeat increases, you will realize that you are running short of breath, which will make you pretty uncomfortable.

- **Exhaustion**

Assuming that one of your significant causes of anxiety is your image, you will find yourself developing negative thoughts because of a poor self-image. You could be walking in the street, and then you turn your head around, catch a glimpse of yourself on a glass wall, and promptly think that something is wrong with you. Then you start to worry that you're looking bad. This causes you to develop self-inhibiting tendencies. When you are obsessed with your image, you tend to do a lot of unnecessary things. You're also trapped in a cloud of intense thought, and you can quickly grow weary as a result.

- **Sleep problems**

For the most part, anxiety makes it hard for you to get sleep. When you have an anxiety trigger, the last thing you want is sleep, until you have resolved your real or imagined problem. So, you lie on your bed, but you don't get a wink of sleep. And knowing the importance of sleep to the overall functioning of the body, you are at a great inconvenience performance-wise. People who have not slept adequately will have trouble performing at work. But then again, anxiety issues can make you sleep excess. Some people who have anxiety imagine that staying in bed and refusing to wake up could make their anxiety go away, which is a misleading idea. To get something done, you must awaken from sleep and actually do it. Spending too much time on your bed will turn you into a non-performer, and at the end of it all, you'll be in a much worse position.

- **Muscle pain**

You have to understand that anxiety induces stress, and the body reacts to stress by tensing up its muscles. If you have a social anxiety disorder, you will probably tend to hold yourself stiff when other people surround you. And when you make this a habit, you will obviously develop muscle pain, which is pretty bad in itself. But then when you have muscle pain, it can restrict you from doing your work properly. If you are a writer, you may have a difficult time sitting down to your laptop and typing up your script. If you are a teacher, you may have a hard time standing before your students and teaching them.

- **Bloating and indigestion**

When one is battling an anxiety disorder, the brain responds by allocating most of the resources to the muscles, so as to either run away from the danger or combat the danger. And as a result, most other critical areas of the body are starved of resources. One of these areas is the stomach. The stomach needs a lot of resources for smooth digestion. But then anxiety makes it hard for the intestines to digest food properly. And this gives rise to both bloating and indigestion. These are pretty much uncomfortable conditions to have. With a bloated stomach, your bowel movement is messed. And with an indigestion problem, you experience stomach pain, which is a profoundly unpleasant condition.

- **Excessive sweating**

One of the most common symptoms of an anxiety disorder is sweating. This is especially so for people who struggle with social anxiety disorder. The mere idea that they have to stand in front of people and speak sends cold shivers down their spine. That's why you might have noticed some people in social gatherings getting wet beneath their armpit or on their backs to the extent that it shows through their shirt. When you have a problem with excessive sweating, it might stop you from leading a healthy life in the sense that it will inconvenience you.

- **Excessive shaking**

Most people with an anxiety disorder find themselves shaking when they are stimulated. For instance, if a person is suffering from a panic disorder, they will find themselves shaking during a panic attack. They might develop panic attacks for flimsy reasons, but still, they'll see themselves shaking. Even people that struggle with social anxiety tend to shake excessively. This stems from their fear of being judged. When you have a tendency to shaking excessively, it denies you the chance to lead a productive life and to enjoy the company of other people without inviting needless scrutiny.

- **Loss of libido**

One of the worst effects of anxiety on physical health is the loss of libido. We all know that one of the pleasures of life is indulging in sexual activity with the person that you prefer. But for you to enjoy this activity, there has to be a sexual fuel, which is pretty much libido. But then anxiety is one of the things that can cause your libido to go down. If you find yourself becoming anxious about sex, you might want to do one or two things that will cause your anxiety to go away. For instance, you might want to start talking with your partner, finding common ground, and see if it will make things any better.

• **Irritability**

Someone that struggles with anxiety might exhibit a habit that will make them pretty much unlikable: being irritable. When someone is easily annoyed, it means they don't want anyone to be around. You would be forgiven to think that this is precisely what they want because they actually resent it. On the one hand, they want people to accept them and like them, but on the other hand, they cannot help but become hostile and irritable. And this causes them to appear like a paradox. In today's world, not many people have the patience to understand what someone is going through; thus, they end up attracting unnecessary hatred.

CHAPTER 8

CBT TECHNIQUES FOR ELIMINATING ANXIETY

There are various Cognitive Behavioral Therapy techniques given to a patient in the context of both therapy and everyday life. These are some of the common techniques that a practitioner may give his patient to overcome anxiety.

- **Skills training**

One of the problems that people have is a lack of skills. When you don't have the right skills, it can be quite problematic. When it comes to anxiety disorders, it is no different. For a person struggling with social anxiety, it may be as a result of simply not having social skills, communication skills, or assertive skills. In order to overcome this challenge, they obviously have to learn the skills. Social skills are not ingrained in one's DNA. It is a pretty much a discipline that anybody can learn as long as they put in the effort. Some very many people might seem charismatic now, even though previously they had been repulsive.

- **Journaling**

This technique is intended to identify what our thoughts and moods are like. Most people tend to act in a reactionary manner without first stopping to understand their thought process. Journaling helps you notice your thoughts and moods, their origin, and their intensity. Let's say that you struggle with post-traumatic stress disorder as a result of losing your marriage. Maybe one day, you are strolling down the road, and you see someone that resembles your ex-partner. Such an instance may trigger an episode of anxiety.

But when you acknowledge that your anxiety stems from that incident, you will be in a much better position to overcome your condition.

- ## Unraveling cognitive distortions

Most people who suffer from an anxiety disorder tend to have a flawed perception of reality. And they get to that point because of their cognitive distortions. These cognitive distortions are merely harmful automatic thoughts. For instance, if you are struggling with social anxiety, you might think that you are ugly, and then try to stay away from people. You might think that by coming close to people, you will expose your weaknesses. But this is just a harmful automatic thought. There are many people with worse features than you that enjoy the company of people. So, when you unravel your cognitive distortions, it means that you will get rid of your harmful automatic thought, and replace it with a positive belief. So instead of thinking yourself ugly, you now start thinking of yourself as beautiful.

- ## Exposure and response

This technique is designed for those who suffer from

obsessive-compulsive disorder. It is technically about exposing yourself to a situation that provokes your compulsive behavior but then restrains yourself from indulging. For instance, if your compulsive habit is checking the door, just sit at the couch, refrain yourself from checking the door once more. You'll feel as though you have to walk up to the door and check it once more, but then remind yourself that you checked it already, and there's no reason for doing that again.

- **Interoceptive exposure**

This technique is used to treat people with panic disorder. It is essentially about helping the patients understand the effects of panic are not necessarily bad. Most people who have panic disorder tend to feel an impending sense of doom, and it is this imagined fear that traps them in this condition. By being put in a situation that elicits their panic and having to sit through the resulting mental activity, it makes them realize that their panic disorder can be very well overcome. For instance, if one of the triggers of their panic disorder is a traumatic event, they can be made to sit through situations that call back those feelings and then confronting those feelings.

- **Nightmare exposure**

This technique is used to help people who suffer from nightmare attacks. It is all about confronting your fears. If a person struggles with nightmares, they may have problems having a quality sleep, which will have a serious impact on the quality of their lives. Nightmare exposure is about creating scenarios that give the subject a nightmare, and once the accompanying emotions come up, the practitioner will help the patient understand their emotions pretty well. In the long run, the patient will understand that nightmares are simply imagined problems.

- **Play the script to the end**

This technique is usually for those who struggle with fear and anxiety. It aims to help the victim understand that fear is only manufactured in their heads. For instance, if you're struggling with social anxiety, you might have developed a habit of avoiding people. This technique aims to put you in a situation that you cannot avoid people, and then you will realize that in the worst-case scenario, nothing terrible will happen. In essence, it is just about conquering your fears. Then the victim realizes that they have only been held back by their fear of the unknown.

- **Progressive muscle relaxation**

This technique is not only used to treat anxiety, but it is an excellent technique also in mindfulness meditation. To eliminate anxiety, it is a very useful technique. Progressive muscle relaxation helps in making a person feel comfortable about themselves. It is about relaxing one muscle group at a time until you experience general comfort in your entire body. You can perform this exercise with the assistance of YouTube videos or audio guidance. This exercise can be incorporated in your daily life for maximum results.

- **Relaxed breathing**

Psychologists believe that one of the ways to fight anxiety is through deep breathing. Whenever you find yourself at the onset of an anxiety attack, just spread out your arms, start drawing in deep breaths. The scientific explanation is that you will take in more oxygen. And with more oxygen going to your brain, you will be in a position to calm down against the situation that elicited your anxiety. With relaxed breathing, all you need is a time commitment, considering that you can do this exercise pretty much anywhere.

Part III

CHAPTER 9

UNDERSTANDING DEPRESSION

D epression is a common mental illness that negatively affects your feelings, thoughts, and behaviors. Pretty much everyone walking the face of the earth has experienced depression. Maybe it came in the form of losing your job, losing your loved one, a sudden breakup, or a streak of bad luck. One thing about depression, when it comes around, you can barely ignore it, for it will stare hard at you until you acknowledge its presence. Depression usually causes the victim to feel sad and to lose interest in the things that they previously found interesting. And then depression reduces one's productivity and affects their ability to function in society.

There isn't always an observable trigger for depression

For most people to become depressed, they can always point to something and consider it as a factor for their depression. It can be an accident, loss of a job, or a social media fight. But then depression can still happen even when everything is seemingly fine. This is because depression can stem from your subconscious mind, being driven by factors that are out of your conscious scope. This means that you cannot always know the cause of your depression unless you enlist the help of mental health professional. Depression has very many faces, and it can be quite hard to understand at first.

Key signs of depression and emotional distress

The first sign is personality change. When someone is struggling with depression, you will notice that their personality has changed. If they used to be happy-go-lucky individuals, they might suddenly become cold. The second sign is agitation. You might notice that person exhibiting unprecedented levels of agitation, which is usually a far cry from what you knew them to be. The third sign is withdrawal. Someone who is struggling with depression rarely wants to be with other people. They will lock themselves in their cave and stay hidden. The fourth sign is poor self-care. Someone who is struggling with depression may stop taking care of themselves because they think too lowly of themselves. Finally, a depressed person loses hope. You will not see them doing the things they are required to do because they have lost all hope.

There is more to depression than sadness

Someone can be sad and not be depressed. Sadness is a common human emotion, and for the most part, it is short-lived. You can be sad now, and a short moment later, you will be joyous. Sadness does not equal depression. In actual fact, some people who go around wearing smiles might be heavily depressed. Depression is, for the most part, a state of being. It causes one to lose interest in the things that they once liked. And it causes them to develop a new attitude about life. If the depression is not checked in time, it can totally ruin a person's life.

Depression can affect children too

There is this myth that depression is an adult's problem. But what many people fail to realize is that depression can affect children too. Children may not have the problems that adults have like financial difficulties, failed relationships, and work-related stress. But that does not mean that childhood is free of any problems. They have their own set of issues, including peer pressure, bullying, and low self-esteem, which can very well trigger episodes of depression. Depression in children is much worse because they don't have the mental capacity to understand what is going on.

It is a real illness

Some people make the mistake of downplaying their depression. As the symptoms become stronger, they may feel like they are becoming crazy, instead of realizing that they need medical help. And such people usually wait until it's too late. In a worst-case scenario, depression can make you descend into the worst habit that you never thought possible. If you have depression and you ignore it, you are at risk of falling from grace to grass. When it comes to eliminating depression, the most important thing is to increase your self-awareness, for then you can recognize the negative thoughts and behaviors.

Depression is treatable

Some people who struggle with depression feel really hopeless because they think there is no cure. Obviously, they are wrong. Depression is a very much treatable illness. The two commonest ways of treating depression are medication and psychotherapy. Both of these avenues of treatment have their pros and cons. But you have to enlist the help of a mental health professional to choose the treatment plan that best suits you. Most people seem to select psychotherapy, and specifically, Cognitive Behavioral Therapy, which is garnering more followers because of its positive impact.

Untreated depression is the leading cause of suicide

People don't merely take their lives because they are experiencing difficulties. There are many people with more challenges than you can imagine, but they would never think of ending life. One of the leading causes of suicide is untreated depression. When a person has lost all hope, it can shut down their critical thinking abilities, and as a result, they might even question the importance of living, which is the line of thought that encourages one to commit suicide. Therefore, it is important to receive help once you realize that you're suffering from depression.

Depression stops you from being sexual

Relationships play an essential role in our lives. If we have strong relationships, it doesn't matter our circumstances, but we will be happy for the most part. In order to keep strong relationships, we must satisfy our partners sexually. It is not reasonable to stay for long stretches of time without indulging in sex with your partner. So, when you find yourself not feeling that urge, you might want to be sure that you are not depressed because depression tends to take away sexual urges. Maybe it is the brain's way of telling you to restore emotional balance first.

Spending all your time with depressed people can make you depressed

To a certain extent, depression is like a cold. You may

catch it from someone who already suffers from it. So, you must be careful about who you spend most of your time with. If you have a tendency to hang out with depressed people, you're most likely going to develop their habits, and in consequence, become just as depressed. But if you're going to hang out with positive people, you will develop a positive mindset, and find yourself acting positively. It might not be easy dissociating yourself from a negative person that you've known all along, but then the alternative is much worse, so you're left with no choice.

Depression can manifest differently in both men and women

In as much as an individual's behavior during depression is tied to their personality, to some extent, a person's sex plays a role. A man and a woman can be both depressed, but there will be a world of difference in how they act. The man might become easily annoyed and withdraw. But the woman is likely to be sorrowful and cling onto their friends.

Exercising can be helpful

When we see someone going to the gym, we might

assume that they're looking for a great shape. There's nothing wrong with having a good shape. But did you know that exercising can also help with depression? Every time you feel low spirited, just put on your training gear and go to the gym. You'll find out that intense workouts tend to fight away the symptoms of depression. But then you must realize that to overcome depression, and you must confront the real issue that is behind your depression. Merely treating the symptoms will not be of help.

Diet can be helpful

Just like exercise, diet can be useful too. Many studies point to the fact that there is a correlation between what we eat and our mental health. If we are used to eating poor diets, we are likely to have poor emotional health. But if we are used to having great diets, we will most certainly have great emotional health. A great diet comprises of various nutrient-dense foods. We must make a habit of consuming these foods.

CHAPTER 10

SYMPTOMS OF DEPRESSION

These are some of the major factors that indicate you're suffering from depression.

- **Hopelessness**

Every person walking the face of the earth aims to achieve something. Their happiness is pegged on achieving that goal. The funny thing about the mind is that as long as you're working toward that goal, your mind will be okay with that.

But once you stop to imagine you can achieve that goal, then it becomes problematic. The moment you become hopeless about life is a clear indication that you are battling a major depressive disorder. Every sane person must keep some hope about a better tomorrow, or about achieving something that they have always looked forward to.

- **Loss of interest**

Have you ever seen someone so interested in a particular hobby, but then at a certain point, they stopped caring about that hobby? It may mean that they got something better to do. But it may also mean that they became depressed. This is what depression does to you. It makes you lose interest in the things that you once liked. So, if you find yourself not being interested in the things that you once loved, you may want to see a mental health professional and ascertain that you don't have depression. Depression is not always loud. It may creep up on you, influencing small parts of your life, until it's too late to salvage the situation.

- **Exhaustion**

It is pretty normal to become exhausted after doing a

physically taxing job. But then if you just woke up from sleep, took your breakfast, and realized you were exhausted, you might be having depression. The mind of the average person with depression tends to be overactive. And this intense mental activity can consume a lot of resources, which leaves the person feeling exhausted. The emotional distress that most people with depression undergo is usually overwhelming. And as a result, the victim feels as if the world is tumbling down on them.

- **Sleep problems**

Another primary symptom of depression is sleep issues. For a well-adjusted person, eight hours of sleep every night are enough. If you find yourself not getting enough sleep or sleeping excessively, you might be having depression. Lack of sleep, or insomnia, can have adverse effects on your life. Since you did not rest enough during the night, you will not have adequate energy to pull through your day. Lack of sleep also makes one irritable, which drives people away from you. Excessive sleep, on the other hand, is just as inadequate. It eats up your productive hours and turns you into a bag of lazy bones.

- **Anxiety**

This condition is characterized by excessive worrying. Most people who struggle with depression tend to be struggling with anxiety too. The average depressed person usually has several cognitive distortions. And since their perception of reality is flawed, the end up being affected by things that don't affect normal people. Anxiety usually causes you to develop self-inhibiting habits that make it hard for you to get along with others. In a worst-case scenario, anxiety causes you to shun other people, as you mislead yourself into thinking that they mean you harm.

- **Changes in appetite**

Some people take to depression by overeating, and others take to depression by abstaining from food, which, in either case, is bad. The person who eats excessively will, without a doubt, gain weight, and if they don't stop themselves, they'll end up becoming obese, which is undesirable. When one becomes obese, they usually develop a negative self-image. And this new development could even worsen their circumstances. On the other hand, when a person stays away from food or eats too little, their body will enter starvation mode, compromising various physiological processes. One should have an average appetite where they eat neither too much nor too little.

- **Unpredictable emotions or no emotions at all**

The scary thing about depression is the fact that it has polar emotional extremes. On the one hand, one might be experiencing unpredictable emotions, so that one moment they might be happy, the next moment they are sad, and then happy again. You never know what to expect with them. But then, in some cases, victims have no emotions at all. They might have a blank expression and the personality of a rock. This lack of emotions is actually scary. A well-adjusted person should be able to show the emotion that they are experiencing.

- **Suicidal thoughts**

Depression is invariably connected with suicidal thoughts. It comes from the fact that you have lost hope. Which means you see no meaning to life. Once you've reached the stage, you might start thinking of ways to end your life. You mislead yourself into thinking that that will help your situation when, in actual fact, it will make your situation even worse, considering the amount of heartbreak you will leave on your loved ones. If you find yourself toying with the idea of suicide, reach out to a mental health professional, because you are clearly suffering from depression.

- **Guilt**

If you've done something terrible, like stealing or killing, it is natural to be guilty. But if you have done nothing and you somehow seem to struggle with feelings of guilt, that's a clear sign that you are struggling with depression. Guilt can stop you from being yourself. It causes you to develop self-inhibiting habits, and in the long run, you stop being yourself. So, when you find yourself feeling guilty, there is no probable cause you might want to seek medical help. Depression has a way of creeping up on someone, making small impacts at first, and once it has taken firm root within you, then the symptoms become far strong.

- **Digestive problems**

This is not to mean that every time you have a digestive problem, you must be suffering from depression. Most of the time, it will be down to your poor eating habits. But then researchers have found that there is a link between digestive problems and depression. If you find that you are experiencing a bloated stomach or indigestion, even when your diet is on point, there is a chance that you could be suffering from depression.

- **Irritability**

This applies especially to men. Most men who struggle with depression tend to become irritable. In other words, they become easily annoyed. Being around them is akin to walking on eggshells. Who wants that? This exactly why people shun them. When you are irritable, it becomes hard to work with another person.

CHAPTER 11

CAUSES OF DEPRESSION

Many people suffer from depression. But then depression can be caused by many different factors. These are some of the common causes of depression.

- **Abuse**

This is one of the leading causes of depression. And it is especially so if one underwent abuse as a child. People who have been abused at one point have a hard time overcoming those nasty feelings. Maybe it was a physical abuse where they were beaten up by their parents or friends. Maybe it was sexual abuse where they were taken advantage of by their partners or even strangers. Or perhaps it was emotional abuse where they were emotionally exploited by people who had authority over them, e.g., Bosses, parents, relationship partners, or even friends. Childhood abuse is the worst. It usually evokes a lot of nasty feelings, and the victim hardly knows how to resolve it, especially if their parents meted the violence.

• Medication

Depression can come about as a result of prescription drugs or self-medication. It is no fault of yours, but just the way it is. This is why you need to always get medical assistance from qualified professionals. They will guide you into receiving proper medication without putting you at risk of developing depression. But then, in some instances, it is unavoidable. The good thing about this kind of depression is that it subsides once the effects of the drugs wear off. And also, ensure that you take prescription drugs without breaking the instructions. An overdose or an under-dose is likely to trigger depression.

• Conflict

Depression may come about as a result of getting involved in many conflicts. You may be having a dispute with your family, friends, colleagues, or even corporations. Ordinarily, both parties antagonize each other, and at the end of the day, no compromise is reached. This constant state of conflict can make you emotionally vulnerable and trigger depression. Thus, you must maintain peace in your life. This is not to mean that you should let everybody through at your expense. You will find yourself needing to make a stand despite the prospect of conflict - and yet that will be the better decision. But then make sure to stay away from conflict if the circumstances allow.

• Loss

Another cause of depression is a loss. As human beings, we tend to be attached to various things or people, and once these things or people are taken away from us, everything goes to hell. Depending on the degree of attachment, loss of a property, or an individual can invite significant grief into our lives, culminating in depression. Does this mean that we should stop being attached to important things or people? By no means! But then you should develop your mental strength so that you·can withstand any kind of loss and not turn into vices as a coping method. I'm sure you have seen so many people who have not recovered since losing their loved ones. They might have turned to alcohol or other drugs in order to numb themselves from the pain.

- **Genetics**

Did you know that depression could be down to your genetics? Researchers have found evidence that some people are genetically predisposed to having depression. So, if you're battling depression at present, and you have it in your DNA, there is a good chance that your offspring will struggle with depression too. When your depression is genetically ingrained, it becomes so much harder to overcome the condition. But even then, all hope is not lost, and there are certain things that you can do to lead a fulfilling life, free of the adverse effects of depression.

- **Major events**

The average person is always looking to make the big step forward, and when it happens, they will quickly share about it on social media. But did you know that significant events can bring about depression? Whether it's a new job, an increase in salary, getting divorced, moving to another country, it comes with a feeling of being overwhelmed, which can very well trigger depression. Does this mean that we should stop making advancements in life? By no means! But we should become alive to the reality that significant events in life can bring about depression, which means we must fortify our mental resources in order to pull through these significant events.

- **Social problems**

When you hear a person saying that they like to stay alone, don't take them for their word. Nobody can withstand complete isolation. Even introverts will need to socialize with other people from time to time in order to feel happy. When someone is having difficulties fitting in society, they can quickly become depressed. This is because human beings are social animals. And there are very many needs that can only be fulfilled in the context of society. Some of the reasons why society might shun someone include performing abominable acts and mental illness.

- **Major illness**

Depression may come about as a result of a major disease. Chronic diseases usually have nasty effects on the sufferer. For instance, asthma causes one to feel tremendous pain. Now you can imagine having to deal with pain for months or even years. It breaks your fighting spirit. And once your hope of getting better is gone, depression sets in. Thanks to heaven, we live in an era where most illnesses can be treated. So, it doesn't matter what you might be suffering from, rest assured there is a way of managing that illness, or at the very least watering down the symptoms.

- **Substance abuse**

When you see someone with an addiction to drugs, what comes to mind? You might probably think that that person is hedonistic? But that is only partly true. The real cause behind addiction is feelings of emptiness and loss of hope. People turn to drugs in order to escape reality. But sadly, that euphoric feeling is only short-lived, which necessitates the addict to increase the dosage. It goes on and on in a negative cycle until the addict is hopelessly buried in the addiction. So, whenever they haven't gotten a fix of their favorite drug, they develop depression.

- **Poor nutrition**

Another cause of depression is poor nutrition. Researchers have found that there is a connection between what we eat and our mental health. If we happen to have a poor diet, our mental health will be just as poor. And if we have a great diet, our mental health will be excellent too. So, make it a habit to consume all the necessary nutrients. Minimize your intake of red meat and sugary drinks. And increase your consumption of vegetables and fruits.

CHAPTER 12

RISK FACTORS FOR DEPRESSION

Depression does not discriminate against age, race, or gender. It affects pretty much everyone. But then there are factors that make a person susceptible to developing depression. These are some of the factors that increase the likelihood of becoming depressed.

- **Low self-esteem**

When we say that a person has low self-esteem, we mean that their self-perception is negative for the most part. They don't think highly of themselves. Such people make good candidates for depression. Low self-esteem not only makes you depressed, but it also takes away all the fun from your life. Most people who struggle with low self-esteem have self-inhibiting tendencies that stop them from realizing their true potential. For instance, one might have a specific talent, but they won't have the courage to take the initiative and see their star shine. They end up becoming another sad case of wasted potential.

- ### Personality disorder

There are many factors that are responsible for success. But if we can name the main one, it has to be personality. This is because real success happens in the context involving many other people. But in order to charm people, you must have a pleasant personality. Everyone is born with a charming personality, but somewhere down the road, we are made to become ashamed of ourselves, and this gives rise to many personality disorders that shun people from us. A personality disorder can very well predispose you to depression. Most people who have personality disorders are acutely aware of it, and there is always an internal conflict going on, which ultimately triggers depression.

- **Financial hardship**

One of the worst challenges to encounter is around money. Most of our needs want, and most definitely, luxuries require money. What happens when you don't have the money to satisfy your needs, let alone your wants? It can be a very unpleasant experience. Financial hardship not only makes your life hard, but it also predisposes you to depression. There are far many people who have taken their lives as a result of not being able to service their loans. Financial misery is one of the worst kinds of pain that someone might face.

- Death of a loved one

Human beings are social animals. We like forming relationships. We feel safe in relationships with the people we love. But then human beings are mortal. So, what happens when the person we loved the most is taken away from us? We feel totally lost. Someone who has lost their loved one is a considerable risk of developing depression. But then you have to remember that death is a natural law, so it cannot be wished away. The only option we have is to toughen ourselves emotionally so that when our loved ones are taken away from us, we won't forever wallow in self-pity, but we will find the courage to move on.

- **Childhood trauma**

Someone who was abused as a child probably holds the most significant risk of developing depression in adulthood. The thing about childhood trauma is that it is always unresolved. When you are a child, you don't have the mind to take the right action. You are literally at the mercy of your tormentor. But then a child has cognition of what is happening to them. Children have a deep awareness of being hurt. They repress those emotions until they are old enough to admit even to themselves that they were I love you abused. Childhood trauma carries a particularly powerful bomb of feelings and resentment.

- **Alcoholism**

One thing you have to remember about alcohol is that it is a depressant. This means that when you take a drink, you are predisposing yourself to a mood of being depressed. It is no wonder that most alcoholics suffer from the worst kind of depression. Any sober moment they will be depressed. So, they have to get drunk in order to forget about their problems. But they can forget about their problems only for so long. So, they have to keep chugging at the alcohol to ensure a permanent state of "bliss" also-known-as insulation from reality.

- **Lack of support**

No human being is an island unto themselves. Every person needs help from others. If a person has become too disappointed by never receiving help from others, they tend to despair, thus inviting depression. The best example of people who easily despair as a result of lacking support is the jobless masses. They think that the "system" has failed them. This is why they tend to develop a bad attitude against any representative of the system. In as much as it is okay to place your hope in people, it doesn't also hurt to develop your self-sufficiency. You cannot be genuinely self-sufficient, but learning survival skills will do you a world of good when the people you expected to come through fail you.

- **Eccentricity**

When I talk about eccentric individuals, I don't really mean those people that defy society to make a statement. They are only eccentric because they have an agenda. I'm talking about those people who are eccentric without even realizing it. For such a person, they might feel as if they are not native to planet earth, because there is nothing about human beings that excites them. They do things in a contrary manner, not because they are looking for attention but because it seems right to them. Naturally, society will be against such people, and it can cause them tremendous emotional distress. If you are an eccentric person, you have to develop the courage to stand for what you believe in, and you must not cower so as to be less intimidating and make people around you comfortable.

- **Eating disorder**

Food plays a significant role in our lives. This is because food nourishes us. You are not supposed to have too much food, and in the same vein, you're not supposed to have too little food. Some people with eating disorders tend to consume very little food, and this not only inconveniences their physiological processes but also predisposes them to depression. Some people also have a tendency to consume foods that are low in nutrients and shunning nutrient-dense foods. Obviously, they are doing a disservice to themselves. Ensure that you have proper eating habits.

CHAPTER 13

NEGATIVE EFFECTS OF DEPRESSION ON PHYSICAL HEALTH

Lack of sleep

When you are depressed, your brain thinks that something is totally wrong, and for that reason, it goes on overdrive, looking for a solution. This alertness can deny your sleep. Most depressed people tend to lie on their bed, and they won't sleep a wink. You can imagine that when this condition is prolonged, all the adverse effects that will come about. Lack of sleep means that one did not rest. And it becomes challenging to take on their traditional roles. Such people find it hard to become productive. And with loss of productivity, they might lose status, and potentially even income.

• Headaches

Some researchers have pointed out that depression is merely the mind's way of communicating an important message. But then this message is not always obvious. So, this might bring about mental unease. In severe cases, one may develop migraines. When you have a headache, you cannot function normally. Headaches tend to make us less critical thinkers, and they take away our capacity to be productive. When you are battling a headache for a long time, it will obviously affect your productivity. Some forms of headaches are life-threatening.

• Chronic pain

When one is depressed, the brain takes it that you are having a tough time of it, and as a result, it sends most of the resources to your muscles. In some instances, it might cause the soreness of muscles. Thus, people who are battling depression tend to struggle with chronic pain. Of course, it becomes hard to be productive and enjoy your life when you are struggling with chronic pain. Also, it is an expensive affair. You not only have to seek help for your depression, but you also have to get rid of chronic pain, which might see you buying various medications.

• Exhaustion

Battling depression is no joke. It uses up a lot of mental resources. Someone battling depression might stay the entire day indoors, and by sunset, they will be exhausted because of thinking too hard. When a person is depressed, he's likely to be overthinking about something, or he may commit his mental resources towards thinking of how to overcome his problem. The brain uses up a lot of resources as it tries to make sense of the depressive state of your mind. It's why you see most depressed people losing weight.

• Stomach problems

Thanks to depression, the brain allocates excessive resources to muscles, in order to aid the fight or flee response. As a result of allocating mot resources to muscles, other essential parts are starved of energy, which invariably affects the working of some body systems. One of these body systems is the digestive system. With most resources allocated to muscles, it becomes hard for the intestines to digest the food as it would have under normal circumstances. And then, as a result, the victim struggles with gastrointestinal problems like bloating and indigestion.

- **Inflammation**

When the brain allocates most resources to muscles, obviously, other organs and body systems are left with little energy to drive them. The immune system relies on body cells in order to fight away infections and protect the body's disease agents. But considering that these body cells have a limited supply of energy, the immune system itself is compromised. As a result, you start to see inflammation, which is a clear sign that the body is being attacked by unwanted disease agents. Inflammation in itself gives a person an unhealthy look and lessens a person's desirability. Certainly, a person with a face chock full of inflammation is not as attractive as a person with a clear face. And let's not lie to ourselves, conventional beauty, which, in no small extent, is aided by clear skin, gets you far.

- **Loss of desire for sex**

In your happy days, making love is second nature to you. Once you see the person that you are sexually attracted to, blood starts rushing to your "private tools of the trade." Nothing wrong with that. It's great for humans to indulge in sex because, apart from being a source of fun, it is also an act that keeps us away from the prospect of extinction of our race, for sex leads to procreation. But then when you are depressed, you have a fragile desire or no desire at all to have sex. As a result of losing your desire to have sex, you might find yourself turning into a cranky man or woman, which is not a desirable place to be.

- **Poor heart health**

Considering that depression puts you on edge, and most resources are sent toward the muscles for fighting or fleeing, as the brain assumes there might be a problem, the heart is put under heavy strain in order to pump blood into the muscles. As a result, there's a rapid heartbeat, which puts the hart of developing heart diseases. The adverse effects of having heart disease are merely tremendous. Heart disease not only stops you from being productive, but it also stops you from enjoying your life because it keeps you from most of the activities you once enjoyed, and should you defy these restrictions, you find yourself at risk of losing your life.

CHAPTER 14

CBT TECHNIQUES FOR ELIMINATING DEPRESSION

Pie chart emotion exercise

When it comes to overcoming depression, you have to master your thoughts and emotions. Most people get ravaged by depression because they have no knowledge of what's going on inside their minds and the cause. With this pie chart exercise, you can be able to identify the various thoughts and emotions triggered by your major depressive disorder, and also identify their sources. It involves literally drawing a pie chart and giving multiple reasons for your thoughts and feelings. For instance, if you notice that you are developing a negative opinion about yourself, thinking yourself unworthy, you may give various reasons as to why you have this line of thought, and also list down the causes of this line of thinking. This exercise will help you understand your emotional makeup.

• Investigate your thoughts

When we are depressed, we are basically experiencing negative and unfavorable thoughts and emotions. The problem with most people is that we don't question the legitimacy of these thoughts and feelings. For instance, I might think to myself, "I'm ugly," and as a result, start avoiding people in an effort not to be seen because I'm ashamed of myself. But then the question is: am I really ugly? By investigating this thought and coming to the conclusion that, indeed, I am not ugly, I will be in a good position to overcome my depression. This is a perfect way of identifying dysfunctional thoughts and developing positive beliefs about yourself.

- **Avoid news**

Your practitioner may warn you against watching the news. Most people report that their confidence and levels of self-esteem shot through the roof once they stopped watching the news. If you have noticed, most news items are negative, and it's no coincidence; it's by design. Network executives are in the business of selling airtime, and in order to attract a broad audience, they know too well that negativity sells. In this age of the internet, all the important news items will always reach you, so there's no need to stay glued to the little box, hearing nonstop negative news. There's too much positive news happening around the world, and even though mainstream media hardly picks up on it, there are websites that handle custom, positive communication, and you might just as well subscribe to such news portal and lend them support.

- **Stop yourself from making negative predictions**

One of the significant ways that depressed people stop themselves from leading a fulfilling life is by making negative predictions about themselves. For instance, if you are expected to make a speech on the coming Sunday, you might say to yourself, "I'm going to flop!" This conditions your subconscious mind for failure. And when you take the podium, you will be closer to failing than winning. Instead of making negative predictions about yourself, teach yourself to make positive predictions, and this will condition your subconscious mind to become a winner.

• Ignoring thoughts

In order to overcome depression, you have to have a pretty good understanding of your thoughts, and by extension, yourself. Depression doesn't respect any person. It can attack you as long as you're walking the face of the earth. So, you may be sitting at your home, trying to get busy with a magazine, when suddenly a jarring thought enters your mind, a spark to get you depressed. What do you do to such a thought? Ignore it! But then you have to increase your self-awareness so that you can get to the point where you can even ignore depression-causing thoughts that you don't acknowledge as your own.

• Know your weaknesses

The importance of understanding your weaknesses is that it allows you to prepare for countermeasures against depression. If you are highly self-aware and not a victim of self-deception, you can easily understand your weaknesses. Let's say you are an introvert. You may have a hard time mingling with other people. But then you are thinking of vying for an elective post, and you will have to mingle with other people; what to do? Just admit to yourself that your weakness is making small talk and then start working on it instead of deceiving yourself that you are awesome at it and then make a fool of yourself. If you're honest with yourself, you will find so many people who will be willing to help you overcome your challenge and start leading your best life.

- **Accept yourself**

Another CBT technique for overcoming depression is merely accepting yourself. Generally, human beings like putting themselves into classes. You might be around certain people that don't consider you one of their kindred. So, what to do? Accept yourself - without apology - for what you are! In the modern era, there have emerged new sex apart from the traditional male and female. They are known as transgenders. If you have observed these people, you may have seen that they personify the idea of being proud of who they are regardless of the hostile world they live in. Develop the mindset that it is okay to not be like everyone else and not hang your head low for shame.

- **Identify your cognitive distortions**

Cognitive distortions are the fuel of most mental illnesses. The victims notice a world that is none existent. And this causes them to develop negative beliefs about themselves. In order to overcome depression, you have to learn to notice and get rid of cognitive distortions. Some of the common cognitive distortions include catastrophizing, overgeneralizing, filtering, black or white thinking, and mind-reading.

- **Develop skills**

People become depressed as a result of not having various vital skills to help them pull along. For instance, if someone gets depressed about their inability to fit in society, they probably lack the social skills required to form relationships with other people. In order to overcome this inconvenience, they have to acquire social skills, which involves learning the ropes and practicing many times over, and once they have perfected how to talk with people, they will have an easy time fitting in society.

Part IV

CHAPTER 15

UNDERSTANDING INSOMNIA

Insomnia is a common sleep disorder that makes it hard for a person to fall or stay asleep. For a person with insomnia, they will experience the following; hardship falling asleep, waking up in the middle of the night and having trouble going back to sleep, waking up very early in the morning, being exhausted upon awakening from sleep.

There are two types of insomnia: primary and secondary insomnia. Primary insomnia occurs when a person is struggling with insomnia that is not the result of other health issues. Secondary insomnia comes about as a result of having other health issues, e.g., Arthritis, HIV, cancer.

About 6% of Americans have insomnia

If you have been struggling with falling or staying asleep, just realize that you are not alone. Statistics show that plenty of Americans tend to struggle with this condition. According to the national institutes of health, up to 6% of Americans are struggling with insomnia. One of the main disadvantages of insomnia is that it affects the productivity of a person. When you're struggling with an inability to fall or stay asleep, you tend to be in a pretty passive state of mind, as opposed to when you have rested well during the night, because it makes you more active.

It can be hereditary

If you struggle with insomnia, look carefully into your family to see who else is struggling with the same condition. Researchers have found strong evidence to suggest that insomnia could be passed down in a family tree. If you are genetically predisposed to develop this condition, it becomes pretty hard to overcome it. But then there are things that you can do in order to overcome this problem. The same study also found out that teens who have insomnia are more likely to develop other mental illnesses like anxiety, depression, and panic disorder.

Animals too can have insomnia

If you thought insomnia is a reserve for human beings, think again. Researchers have found evidence that animals, also, can develop insomnia. Researchers bred insomniac animals. They found out that they exhibited similar traits to insomniac human beings. But for the animals that had insomnia, it was clear that their quality of life was low, and they tended to lose balance, learned at a slower pace than other well-adjusted animals, and developed more fat than animals that had healthy sleeping habits. Animals that have insomnia obviously jeopardize their lives, which may not necessarily be the case for humans.

Insomnia can lead to weight gain

People who have trouble falling and staying asleep are at a greater risk of gaining weight than people who observe healthy sleeping habits. The scientific explanation is that insomnia can have a negative impact on the absorption of food, and as a result, more energy is turned into fat. Obviously, gaining weight is not a desirable thing. It reaches a point, and you become obese. Being obese is harmful to your health and your social market value. People who are an overweight struggle with a negative self-image, which usually affects their self-esteem.

Unpredictable sleep schedules can cause insomnia

Insomnia might come about as a result of having unpredictable sleep schedules. Maybe during the week, you had been sleeping at a certain time. And then you got to the weekend, and you began to sleep much later. This difference in sleep schedule can trigger insomnia. If you want to keep insomnia at bay, ensure that you always sleep at the same time. When you condition your body to sleep at a specific time, it becomes easier for you to fall and stay asleep. But if you have an unpredictable schedule for your nights, you'll find yourself having difficulties on how to get asleep.

Sleeping pills won't help

For some reason, when a person won't fall asleep, the rush to their favorite chemist and buy some over-the-counter drugs for sleep. Studies have shown that these drugs are not effective in inducing sleep. But for some strange reason, people won't stop buying these drugs. Insomnia usually comes about as a result of poor habits. This means before you overcome insomnia, you may have first to kick away your poor habits. For instance, if you have a habit of drinking coffee before sleep, you may have to stop doing that, or if your sleep schedule is disrupted, you may want to make it a little steadier.

More women experience insomnia than men

Researchers have found that more women tend to struggle with insomnia than men. But then it is influenced by changes in hormones. 80% of pregnant women reported having poor sleep habits, with loss of sleep being the main issue. Women who had hit menopause also experienced insomnia, and researchers attributed it to their erratic hormones.

It can cause death

In rare instances, a prolonged case of insomnia can lead to death. Researchers attribute this condition to an abnormal protein that develops as a result of a genetic mutation. This protein affects brain function. It causes the victim to lose memory and lose control over the movement of their muscles. The victim also develops hallucinations. For a person who has fatal familial insomnia, they usually start by getting about an hour of sleep every night, accompanied by nightmares. But then it reaches a certain point, and they stop having any sleep at all. This condition brings about extreme fatigue, body tremors, and difficulty in breathing. In the long run, the victim's body is unable to withstand all these nasty conditions, and he passes away.

CHAPTER 16

SYMPTOMS OF INSOMNIA

If you have been struggling with insomnia, these are some of the things that you will experience.

- **Difficulty falling asleep at night**

You may spend the whole day being busy, hoping that when night comes, you will just hit the sheets and drift to sleep. But when you climb onto your bed, nothing happens. You might try to do something extra like reading a book, hoping that will attract sleep, but then it's not enough to get you asleep. You spend the night basically turning and tossing. Apart from the sore muscles, it can put a heavy strain on your emotional makeup. Sleep is something that is incredibly freeing, and being unable to fall asleep can make you extremely uncomfortable.

- **Waking up during the night**

For some people who manage to get asleep, it does not last throughout the night. At some point during the night, the person will awaken. Obviously, this is a very distressing thing.

- **Waking up too early**

Most people who struggle with insomnia tend to wake up early than everybody else. This is down to the fact that they have little sleep, and in the early dawn, they'll be already awake.

- **Exhaustion after sleep**

You would think that after sleeping, one would have rested enough; at least that is what happens to ordinary people. You jump into bed when you're tired, and you wake up when you're refreshed. But for someone struggling with insomnia, they tend to wake up feeling exhausted.

- **Anxiety**

Most people that struggle with insomnia tend to battle anxiety too. So, at night, he will have trouble falling asleep, and during the day, he will be too tense, thanks to his anxiety. In that sense, insomnia can really make a person's life unbearable.

- **Irritability**

For a person who's getting little to no sleep, you do not expect them to be joyous. For the most part, they will be irritable. This means it can be pretty hard to get along with them. They might come off as uptight and arrogant, but the real issue is that they are not getting enough sleep.

- **Daytime tiredness**

When you look at most people who are productive during the day, you can be almost certain about one thing; they had a good night's sleep. But for someone who struggled to get sleep, they'll be practically tired during the day. The human body is not robotic, after all.

• Depression

You will never run into a person that says great things about their insomnia. When a person is incapable of getting sufficient sleep, they usually mourn about it. As time progresses, it may give rise to depression. It is effortless for a person struggling with insomnia to lose hope about life.

• Lack of concentration

At night when one is asleep, their brain is refreshed. This allows them to receive new information in the following day with relative ease. Concentration comes to them quite naturally. But when someone has not gotten enough sleep, first they'll be irritable, and then they'll not have sufficient mental resources to concentrate. And this obviously affects their performance.

• Increased errors

When someone has had a good night of rest, they are likely to be in their element the next day, and this usually minimizes or eliminates all chances of making errors. But when someone does not have enough sleep, they'll be exhausted the next day, and this will make them unable to focus, and as a result, the count of errors will be pretty high.

- **Ongoing worries about sleep**

The mere fact that one cannot get enough sleep is enough to cause one to worry. People that struggle with insomnia have a tendency to worry excessively about their inability to fall asleep. This constant worry usually has a negative effect on their lives.

CHAPTER 17

CAUSES OF INSOMNIA

Insomnia is one of the worst conditions that a human being can ever face because, quite honestly, nothing beats the ecstasy of a good night's sleep. But in order to overcome your insomnia, you have to understand its causes first. These are some of the factors that cause insomnia.

- **Stress**

So many people walk around, claiming that they are stressed. Stress can come from very many things that we are involved in. It can come from our jobs, our relatives, or even friends. But then, having to deal with stress on a constant basis might predispose us to insomnia. What usually happens is that we develop rigid ways of thinking, and as we ponder how to overcome our stressful living conditions, it often stops us from a leading quality and productive life. And being stuck in such a condition can increase our likelihood of developing insomnia.

- **Excessive travel and unpredictable work schedules**

We live in an era where the world has been reduced into a mere village. People are traveling non-stop all around the world. But did you know that jet lag can induce insomnia? This is not to mean that you should not travel at all. But then you might want to take considerable breaks so that you can not only rest but also focus on other dimensions of your growth. We even live at a time when people are extra ambitious. Certain people have a tendency of working long shifts, burning the midnight oil in order to accomplish their essential life goals. But then they fail to notice that long shifts and having unpredictable sleep schedules Karen white insomnia into their lives.

- ### **Poor sleep habits**

This is perhaps the most significant cause of insomnia. Most people have various habits that stop them from experience and quality sleep at night. The first major bad sleep habit that people have is drinking stimulating beverages before bed. The most common is coffee. When you have coffee before you sleep, you are obviously going to have a rough night because coffee is a stimulant. Another poor sleep habit that people have is turning their bed into a workstation. It doesn't matter how you try to rationalize it, but when you turn your bed into a workstation, you are conditioning yourself to fight away sleep. Eating while in bed is another poor habit. It not only promotes laziness, but it also encourages you to eat more than your fill. Another poor habit is a tendency of watching tv or listening to the radio. Both of these activities are stimulating to the mind, and they'll make it hard for you to fall asleep.

- ### **Overeating at night**

Having a light meal is okay. But when you develop a

tendency of consuming too much food right before sleep, it can predispose you to insomnia. When you are heavy in the stomach, you are likely to feel uncomfortable, and for that reason, you will have significant trouble falling asleep.

- **Mental health issues**

Another cause of insomnia relates to mental health issues. When a person is struggling with mental illnesses like anxiety and PTSD, they are likely to develop insomnia. Being mentally ill is no joke. It causes one to stay awake, thinking of how to overcome their condition. Their emotional instability doesn't help matters.

- **Medication**

The problem with the medication is that it brings about many side effects. And it can be pretty hard to live with these side effects. Certain drugs have side effects that make it hard for the patient to get any sleep. But then, if one is not hooked on these drugs for a prolonged period, it is easier to wait out the side effects.

CHAPTER 18

RISK FACTORS FOR INSOMNIA

Advanced age

A person who's 50 years old is more likely to develop insomnia as opposed to a teenager. But this is not to meant that every older person is struggling with a lack of sleep. It is totally possible to be old and enjoy a great sleep every night. You only have to maintain good habits.

- **Chronic illnesses**

The chronic illness tends to hang on for a pretty long

time. One of the most common forms of chronic illness is cancer. When you acquire this illness, you usually end up having to take heavy medication, which can have serious side effects. Chronic illness is one of the factors that increase a person's likelihood to develop insomnia.

- **Medication**

Most of us tend to think that we can self-medicate. For instance, if we are struggling with a headache at present, instead of visiting a doctor and sharing about our problem, we may run to the nearest chemist and buy some drugs. The problem with this action is that we have no special knowledge of these drugs, and they could put us at risk of developing insomnia.

- **Gender**

Researchers have found that women are at a greater risk of developing insomnia than men. Hormones are one of the major factors that increase women's likelihood of developing insomnia. Researchers found out that pregnant women or menopausal women tended to struggle more with lack of sleep thanks to their unpredictable hormones.

- **Psychological issues**

A person who's struggling with many psychological issues is more likely to develop insomnia as opposed to a person who's emotionally well-adjusted. Psychological issues might stem from a number of things like one's social status add financial abilities. Someone with weak psychology is far likely to develop insomnia.

- **Lifestyle**

If someone has a tendency of drinking alcohol late into the night, they are more likely to develop insomnia as opposed to a person whose lifestyle is pretty much standard, meaning that they don't go out late steak and drowning in beer. But then this is not to mean that every person that drinks beer suffers from lack of sleep.

- **Unpredictable shifts**

We may have made significant technological advancement, but not to the point that we do not need human beings anymore to work. Most economies are slowly becoming 24/7 in our economies. So, you find that some people alternate between working during the day and working during the whole of the night, which me to throw their circadian rhythm off the tracks. It is important to have a consistent work schedule so that you can be able to sleep at the same time every day.

- **Jet travel**

There is nothing wrong at all with climbing into a jet and traveling the world. But then researchers have found out that excessive traveling can predispose one to insomnia. This is not to discourage anyone from traveling extensively, calling attention to the nature of what they might have to deal with.

- **Poor sleep environment**

Imagine that you have to sleep on a king-size Arabian bed. You would feel pretty nice, and fall asleep much quicker than you imagined. But then also believe that you have to sleep on the floor on a bug-infested mattress. It would be extremely hard to get sleep in such conditions.

CHAPTER 19

NEGATIVE EFFECTS OF INSOMNIA ON PHYSICAL HEALTH

Pain

One of the effects of insomnia is having to struggle with a sore body. When we sleep, the body undergoes cell regeneration. The weak cells are gotten rid of. This allows the person to be healthy and refreshed. But for a person who's not getting any sleep, they obviously won't benefit from this. So, they tend to struggle with feelings of soreness in various body parts.

- **Headache**

If you go for a few days without sleep, you will undoubtedly come down with a headache. A human being is not designed to stay without sleep. During the night, the brain freshens up, meaning that it casts away the unwanted emotions. This is why when a person wakes up, they always feel fresh. When you don't get any sleep, you will find yourself struggling with headaches.

- **Slurred speech**

Have you ever come across someone who's drunk too much alcohol? Their speech is usually slurred. It is not different from someone who's sleep-deprived. They experience difficulties in forming a coherent sentence. And it can be pretty hard for them to think through what they are saying.

- **Poor balance**

Another negative effect of insomnia on physical health is a poor balance. Most people who are struggling with insomnia tend to have a hard time walking along steadily or even taking a power pose. This is because the part of the brain responsible for balance is somewhat compromised.

- **Poor vision**

For someone who has had a good night's sleep, they won't be having any problems with their eyes. This is because they are in a new mental state. But for someone who is sleep-deprived, their eyelids will be heavy, and they will have a lot of difficulties seeing what is around them.

- **Loss of intelligence**

Researchers have confirmed that the brain is more active during the night than during the day. It engages in the creation of more brain cells, thus improving one's intelligence. But when a person goes for days on end without any sleep, it weakens the brain, and ultimately it makes them dumber.

- **Accelerates aging**

It's not like there's anything wrong about aging, but you don't want to be growing old much faster than usual. People who receive adequate sleep tend to age at a standard rate. In some instances, it is believed quality asleep can slow down aging. So, when you go for days on end without a wink of sleep, you're only asking to look older than you really are.

- **Kills sex drive**

Another problem with sleep deprivation is that it takes away your desire to engage in sexual activity with other people. Now, this is a significant problem. A healthy person should have a sufficient libido because wanting to have sex is pretty much natural. But then insomnia tends to take away that desire.

- **Increases your likelihood of developing other health conditions**

Not only insomnia leaves you feeling weary, but it can increase your risk of developing other physical illnesses. Researchers have found that most people who have insomnia also tend to battle other illnesses on the side. Some of these illnesses include heart attack, diabetes, and stroke.

- **Poor memory**

People who are used to getting adequate sleep tend to have a relatively stable memory. This is because their brain can develop more cells during sleep. But then people who struggle with sleep deprivation have a hard time remembering things. Having a poor memory can be pretty inconveniencing.

- **It can make you obese**

Researchers have found a connection between lack of sleep and increased hunger. So, if you have a tendency of going for days on end without getting any sleep, you may find yourself eating a lot more than usual. In the long run, you will end up piling on weight until you are obese.

CHAPTER 20

CBT TECHNIQUES FOR ELIMINATING INSOMNIA

For some reason, most people seem to attempt to treat their sleep deprivation by swallowing pills. It has long been established that pills don't help. But this is not mean that there are no other ways of treating sleep deprivation. One of the best ways of overcoming insomnia is through Cognitive Behavioral Therapy. The following are some of the CBT techniques that help in overcoming insomnia.

- **Stimulus control therapy**

This technique is aimed at eliminating factors that set your mind to resist sleep. The practitioner might ask you to set consistent sleep time and wake time and avoid taking naps during the day. This technique requires that you use your bed for only sleeping. If you climb onto your bed and for some reason, the sleep won't come, you should go to some other room, and only come back when you are feeling sleepy.

- **Alcohol avoidance**

If you have a tendency to drink alcohol late into the night, you will find yourself struggling with sleep issues. Alcohol tends to influence your nervous system, and it becomes hard for you to get sleep. This technique aims at keeping you away from alcohol so that you can be pretty sober when you go to sleep.

- **Caffeine avoidance**

Like alcohol, caffeine is just as bad. People that drink caffeine a few hours before they go to sleep will experience difficulties getting sleep. The practitioner might ask you to stay away from caffeine a few hours before you sleep. This means you will not be stimulated, and sleep will come to you much more naturally.

- **Improving hygiene**

In some instances, sleep deprivation might be tied to poor hygiene. Can you imagine having to sleep in a dusty, bug-infested bed? Anyone would have trouble closing their eyes. But when you clean up your bedroom and use clean sheets and mattress, it becomes a lot easier to fall asleep.

- **Improving the environment**

Another way to fight sleep deprivation is through making improvements in an individual's sleeping environment. This means you only have to keep the necessary things in the bedroom and get rid of the unnecessary stuff. It may not be easy because you may have developed an attachment to various things. For instance, the tv and radio have to go.

- **Relaxation**

This technique aims to make a person feel more relaxed. You're obviously not going to fall asleep if you're feeling tense most of the time. But then relaxing helps you fall asleep much faster. This technique involves things like meditation, imagery, and deep breathing exercises.

- ## Paradoxical intention

In this technique, a patient has to fight away the fear of not being able to sleep. Usually, what happens with people who have insomnia, they will throw themselves onto the bed, and start worrying that they're not falling asleep. But this technique is designed to make a person resist that kind of worrying.

- ## Biofeedback

This technique aims to keep watch over your heart rate and muscle tension and show you how to adjust them. Your professional mental health assistant will hand you a device for taking various measures. This will help you understand how your body is responding to the environment.

Part V

CHAPTER 21

UNDERSTANDING STRESS

S tress is basically how the body reacts to changes that require you to make an adjustment. It is a self-preserving reaction aimed at protecting you from potentially harmful scenarios. Stress is very much a regular thing. It can stem from almost anywhere.

Everyone is affected by stress

Both the king of the world and the poorest have one thing

in common; they all get stressed. Nobody is ever safe from feeling stressed. But then how you responded to this stress makes all the difference. An inadequate response to stress can predispose you to be physical and mental illnesses. But then again, stress can be the catalyst that pushes you to become an overachiever.

Not all stress is bad

The funny thing about your subconscious mind is that it reads into environments way before you consciously think about what is happening. For instance, if you are in a potentially dangerous situation, you will feel stressed, and as a result, your brain will furnish your muscles with the resources it requires to fight or flee. That is why you hear people saying that when they were running away from danger, they don't know how they gathered that kind of speed.

Long-term stress can be perilous

Even though we are saying that not all stress is bad, if you experience stress on a long-term basis, it can have a negative impact on your health. Chronic stress usually suppresses the immune system, digestive system, and reproductive system. So, if you have been suffering from stress on a long-term basis, you should increase commitment to eliminate it, lest it does you harm.

Stress can be managed

Just because you're feeling stressed, it doesn't mean that you're helpless. There are various things that you can do to manage stress. The most important thing is to have the self-awareness to understand what is triggering your stress. When you know clearly the origin of your stress, it becomes so much easier to overcome it. Some of the common ways of managing stress include; talking to your friends, exercising, relaxation, setting goals for yourself.

It is okay to ask for help from a professional

Most of the time, people who are stressed tend to keep it to themselves. They imagine that stress is something to be ashamed of. But that's the wrong mentality. It is totally okay to step out and look for professional help. Actually, it is far more beneficial to look for professional advice the instant you feel stressed. Mental health experts will help you overcome your stress.

A bad attitude worsens stress

If you have a poor attitude, you're in for a rough ride. Almost everyone has reasons to be stressed. But the real test is in the attitude that you keep while managing your stress. For instance, if you decide to take it out on innocent people, you are only inconveniencing yourself and putting your reputation on the line. Life will not always be rosy. But through emotional intelligence, we can manage to avoid falling victim to stress.

Excessive stress can accelerate your aging process

You must have heard that if you want to stay young, you must avoid stress at all costs. There is a lot of truth in that statement. Most people who suffer from stress are good at repressing it. For that reason, their minds are always racing, and it causes them to have a weary look, thus hastening their aging process.

Vices are not helpful

Some people tend to react to stress by turning to vices or developing addictions. One of the most common forms of addictions that people acquire as a result of stress is smoking. Some people think that by smoking they'll keep stress at bay. Although smoking can make you feel great for a little while, the negative long-term effects are not worth it, because they actually make your stress even worse. Some other people turn to other addictions like sex, partying, and video games. All of this is an attempt to run away from reality, which is pointless.

CHAPTER 22

SYMPTOMS OF STRESS

The following are some common symptoms that nearly every stressed person may experience.

- **Agitation**

Someone who is experiencing stress will always have the look of being agitated. And this is especially true if they've not mastered their emotions. Being agitated all the time can cause people to stay away from you. This partly explains why stressed people tend to be lonely.

• Being overwhelmed

When a person is experiencing stress, they feel as though their life is running out of control. They tend to struggle with feelings of being overwhelmed. And this is usually seen in the lowering of their productivity. When a person is overwhelmed for so long, they might become disorientated about life.

• Difficulty relaxing

A stressed person will hardly be relaxed. They tend to have so many worries. And as a result of these worries, it becomes hard for them to lead a fulfilling life. Being relaxed is all about reaching a great state of mind in spite of your circumstances. But most stressed people cannot afford to be relaxed because they imagine that the worst is up.

• Low self-esteem

Most stressed people tend to struggle with feelings of low self-esteem. They may develop a negative self-image. And this causes them to develop self-inhibiting habits. They might be very talented, but talk themselves down, that's discouraging themselves from taking action and becoming shining stars. Low self-esteem creeps into virtually every area of their life.

- ## Avoiding other people

Someone who is battling stress might think that something is wrong with them. They might believe that stressful scenarios occur only in their lives because they deserve it. But if they had known better, they would understand that stress happens to almost everyone. So, this flawed perception causes them to avoid other human beings, which is sad, considering that no one can exist without relying on other human beings.

- ## Low energy

What you first notice about a stressed person is that their productivity takes a hit. Stress seems to have a slowdown effect on the workings of the brain. It virtually holds the brain captive. And as a result, the victim channels all their resources towards solving their stress, which leaves them feeling low energy.

- ### Rapid heartbeat

Some people experience an increase in a heartbeat when they are struggling with stress. You have to understand that the brain's interpretation of stress is that that person is in danger. So, the body reacts by supplying nutrients to muscles so as to aid the fight or flight response. But for this to take place, the heart tends to be overworked, thus resulting in an increased heartbeat.

- ### Clenched jaw and grinding teeth

This usually happens in situations where a person is not only stressed but mad about it. Let's say you are a parent. One day you go to pick up your kid from school, except you find that your kid is not there. Chances are, you will not only become stressed but also angry about it. In such a situation, you might start clenching your jaw and grinding your teeth.

- ### Constant worrying

For someone who's struggling with stress, they are always looking at what might or might not happen. Going back to the example above, if you realized that your kid was not in school, you may start worrying about what could have happened to them. But then constant worrying doesn't help matters. In actual fact, it makes things even worse.

• Forgetfulness and disorganization

When a person is stressed, their memory takes a hit. This is usually because of their racing thoughts. Such a person will find himself thinking from many dimensions about their stressful conditions. This can have a negative impact on their ability to remember things. Stressed people also tend to be more disorganized. For the most part, they are mainly concerned about overcoming their stress, but other things become secondary.

• Lack of focus

A stressed person will have a hard time concentrating on a task. Their mind is preoccupied with their stressful conditions, leaving them with no mental resources to channel to what they are doing. Most stressed people struggle with racing thoughts that keep them from concentrating on what they're doing.

- **Poor judgment**

This does not happen because they have mental retardation, but it happens merely because they're not paying enough attention. Most stressed people already have a lot in their mind. So, they can be a bit overwhelmed when it comes to making new decisions, especially if these decisions require a bit of critical thinking.

CHAPTER 23

CAUSES OF STRESS

These are some of the factors that might cause one to develop stress.

- **Loss of a loved one**

Human beings are social animals. Much of our happiness is tied to our excellent relationships with other people. If you are intimate with a person, you might have become attached to them. But then when you lose them, you might be unable to overcome the pain, thus becoming stressed throughout.

- **Divorce**

Inasmuch as we rely on other human beings to be happy, these relationships don't always have a happy ending. No marriage is ever safe from the idea of divorce, no matter how long they have been together. But one thing is sure; divorce shatters the partners emotionally. So, if you have experienced a divorce, you might be stressed, which is quite reasonable.

- **Financial hardship**

Some people say that money is the only thing that matters. Most things in your life might not be working, but as long as you have money, you can afford the comforts that the world has to offer. For a person who is experiencing financial hardship, they don't have the means to acquire what they want, and this can bring them a lot of grief.

- **Getting married**

You might think that now someone has gotten a life partner, they'll break into song and dance about it. But the actual truth is that this is a very overwhelming event. Getting married is basically selecting someone that you will grow old up with. And knowing the true nature of human beings is that they always have doubts. So, someone might stress about their choice.

- ## Moving to a new home

Another thing that tends to invite stress is moving to a new place. If there is one property that human beings are attached to is their home. That is why most people carefully think through their decision before they decide to buy a house. But it seems the analysis is never quite over. When someone moves to a new home, they might experience racing thoughts, perhaps wondering whether they made the right decision, which can cause them tremendous stress.

- ## Chronic illness

When someone is suffering from a chronic illness, they are almost always experiencing pain. Whether it is in the form of headaches, chest pain, or joint pain, none of those is desirable. Chronic illnesses also make the sufferer feel bad. And all of these adverse effects come together and make the person feel stressed.

• Depression

A depressed person has virtually lost hope. Think about a beautiful woman who's looking to get a career in the modeling industry. They have to go through many trials. The rejection is painful. But as long as she thinks that she stands a chance of winning a contract, she will always feel good about herself. But when she loses hope, she will undoubtedly suffer from depression. And one of the main symptoms of depression is excessive stress.

• Taking care of the elderly or children

The average human being has a destructive force that can be quite challenging to tame. Think about the kids. They are full of energy and ideas. They are always thinking up new ways to cause trouble. And the same is not different for the elderly. If you're given the job of looking after vulnerable people, you can quickly become stressed, especially because you cannot get to reason with them.

• Traumatic event

Let's say one day you were driving down the road.

Suddenly a car veered off its lane and slammed into you. But by some stroke of luck, you survived. When you revisit that traumatic experience, it could be enough to get your stressed. You might find yourself thinking back to the trauma or experiencing flashbacks and visions, but none of them is pleasant.

- **Work-related stress**

Our work plays a significant role in our lives. This is where we get our income. But even more importantly, this is where we spend most of our productive hours. But then the workplace can be a source of tremendous stress, especially when you consider the fact that most people don't love their jobs. Some of the things at your workplace that may induce stress include; being unsatisfied with your job, having a hostile boss, having a lot of responsibilities, working long shifts, working in poor conditions, dealing with hostile or negative colleagues, and dealing with discrimination.

CHAPTER 24

RISK FACTORS FOR STRESS

Age

It is true that stress comes to all. Both the young and old equally get stressed. But when you look at it closely, you realize that the more advanced of age you are, the more likely you are to come down with stress. For one, as an older person, you have been into many things and activities that have transformed into sources of stress. But even though the kid will get stressed too, they don't have a lot of life experience. Or in other words, they don't have opportunities for getting stressed as much as adults do.

- **Substance abuse**

If you have a tendency to abuse drugs, you are at much more risk of developing stress as opposed to a person who is sober. Substance abuse makes a slave out of you. The moment that you will fail to get your fix, it can become deeply problematic for you to function. That is why you see people who are addicted to drugs tend even to shake when they don't get their fix.

- **Low self-esteem**

When you have low self-esteem, it means that you don't think highly of yourself. It means that you let other people through at your expense. People with low self-esteem are more likely to get stressed than people who are self-confident. This is because there's always a clash between what they want and how they act. People with low self-esteem have a difficult time saying "no" to others, and this causes them to be taken advantage of, and in the long run, it causes them to experience even more stress.

- **Personality**

Did you know that your character can predispose you to stress? Let's say you are an introvert, but you work around extroverts. Maybe you want to be friendly, and you never tell them that you hate being surrounded by loudmouth. In as long as you want to mind your business, you find it hard, because your personality does not rhyme with the other people's personality. And this can cause you to become stressed.

- **Environment**

Someone who stays in a quiet, posh area with loving parents is more likely to be mentally stable as opposed to someone who lives in a chaotic part of town where strife is the order of the day. The environment that you live in plays a major role in your emotional makeup. If you are surrounded by troublemakers, there's a high chance that you will become a troublemaker yourself.

CHAPTER 25

NEGATIVE EFFECTS OF STRESS ON PHYSICAL HEALTH

Headache

The most common effect of stress on people is a headache. When someone is experiencing stress, their thoughts tend to race, but they never seem to get a solution. And this disappointment can trigger a headache. Let's revisit the example that you went to school to pick up your kid and found that they were not there. You start wondering where they might be. But you don't get an obvious answer. At that point, you may begin to experience a headache because you don't know what to do next.

- **Muscle pain**

When you experience stress, your brain reacts by activating your fight or flee response. It does so by sending a lot of the body's resources to your muscles so as to increase your survival chances. But this very response might leave your muscles sore. And of course, pain is pretty inconveniencing. With sore muscles, you will definitely find it hard to do normal things, and you may want to stay a lot longer in your bed, which obviously affects your productivity, and by extension, your earning potential.

- **Chest pain**

When one is experiencing stress, the brain sends a lot of resources to the muscles. In that sense, the heart is very much involved, because it is the organ that pumps blood around. Firstly, the heartbeat goes up, and then one might find himself dealing with chest pain.

- **Fatigue**

Being stressed comes at a great emotional cost. Their minds tend to be overactive. They are always thinking of ways to overcome their stressful conditions. But then this constant struggle to overcome their stress will deplete their energy reserves. And they end up feeling exhausted.

- **Sleep problems**

When you have stress, you cannot relax enough to fall and stay asleep. You spend most of your waking hours wondering about how to overcome your stress. And when night comes, your overactive mind makes it hard for you to sleep. If you manage to fall asleep, it is essentially one rocky ride throughout the night.

CHAPTER 26

CBT TECHNIQUES FOR ELIMINATING STRESS

Cognitive Behavioral Therapy techniques can be used both in the context of therapy and in everyday life. Either way, it's a win. The following techniques are designed to help you overcome your stress.

- **Journaling**

This technique might seem simple, but it is actually very useful. It is all about writing down your experiences, emotions, and thoughts. Whenever you find yourself struggling with stress, take your diary and write down various things about your condition. Writing down your thoughts not only helps you calm down, but it gives you a new perspective. If you have been stressed throughout the most part of the day, take out your diary and write down the various triggers for your stress. Maybe it was your boss or your colleagues. Write down how you felt about it. And if you have any solution, write it down too.

- **Unravel your flawed perceptions**

Sometimes we get stressed unnecessarily. This usually comes about as a result of believing something that is not true. Assuming that you're looking for work, and one of your core beliefs is that you are stupid, every rejection letter that you get will cement your flawed belief. If you go around thinking that you're silly, you will develop self-inhibiting tendencies, and you will have a hard time accomplishing your goals.

- **Expose yourself to your fears**

One thing about human beings is that there's no limit to

how powerful you can be. You are literally as powerful as you want to be. If you are an introvert, you can very well learn to be around extroverts, as long as you put in the effort. Learn to overcome your stress but putting yourself in challenging situations.

- **Progressive muscle relaxation**

This technique is aimed at making you feel more relaxed. It involves relaxing one muscle group at a time until your whole body attains a state of relaxation. If you're not skilled in this, there are very many resources to help you, especially on YouTube. Whenever you feel stressed, look for a quiet place, put on some soothing music, and get started relaxing your muscles.

- **Deep breathing**

Did you know that you can overcome your stress by drawing in deep breaths? When you draw in a lungful of breath, you are putting more oxygen into the body. And with more oxygen, the brain gets more fuel, which aids in formulating a solution. So, whenever you find yourself getting stressed, stop whatever you're doing, and start drawing in and out deep breaths. It will leave you feeling relaxed and free of stress.

CHAPTER 27

HOW COGNITIVE BEHAVIORAL THERAPY HELPS TREAT POST-TRAUMATIC STRESS DISORDER

Post-traumatic stress disorder (PTSD) is a mental illness that's triggered by an unpleasant experience. The experience causes you to endure flashbacks, and nightmares, as you relive the horrible event, causing PTSD.

Most people who experience traumatic events usually have a difficult time adjusting and moving on with their lives, but eventually, they manage to adapt and carry on. But if the debilitating anxieties and flashbacks carry on for months or years, you certainly have the condition known as post-traumatic stress disorder (PTSD).

Symptoms of PTSD

The symptoms of post-traumatic stress disorder might show up as early as a month within the traumatic event, but in some instances, the symptoms can wait for years. Post-traumatic stress disorder hinders you from living a normal life and causes significant problems, especially on your social life, work-life, and relationships. The following are the four categories of PTSD symptoms:

- Intrusive remembrances
- Avoidance
- Negative changes in thoughts
- Altered physical and emotional reactions

Intrusive remembrances

If you had healed from a traumatic event, your mind wouldn't go back to relive the horrible experience. However, for someone with PTSD, their brain tries to get them to relive the horrible experience in a myriad of ways. The affected person starts experiencing vivid flashbacks, which obviously ruin their mental stability. They may also begin to experience nightmares on a frequent basis, and these nightmares are related to the horrific event. Additionally, the person experiences severe distress when they run into things that are associated with the traumatic event. For instance, if a young woman was raped at night, she may get severely distressed every time she passes through the exact spot she had been raped, calling to mind the horrible details.

Avoidance

It's human nature to want to avoid confronting things that have traumatized you, but then a well-adjusted person shouldn't have any difficulty revisiting their past when there's an incentive. A person afflicted with PTSD totally avoids speaking about their traumatic past. In fact, they might not take it kindly if someone approaches them, wanting to find out about their trauma. They will also go to great lengths to avoid people, things, or situations that are associated with the horrific event, considering that these things could trigger nasty memories.

Negative changes in thoughts

People living with PTSD develop negative thought patterns about themselves or the world. For instance, they may consider themselves as worthless, develop an inferiority complex, and develop a deep-seated hatred against the world as a whole. They see the world as being against them. They also tend to become hopeless, and it discourages them from making any bold steps since they don't believe they can achieve anything. Their memory becomes stunted, especially concerning various aspects of the traumatic event. Since they hate the world, they have extreme difficulties starting and maintaining relationships, and alienate themselves from those that care about them, for instance, friends and family. They lose interest in activities that they once enjoyed and also have a hard time feeling positive emotions.

Altered physical and emotional reactions

After you have gone through a traumatic event, you might become a little more cautious and sensitive, but that tendency eventually goes away as you adjust. However, when your reflexes continue to be amazingly active so that you are easily startled or frightened, it is indicative of PTSD. People with PTSD seem to be always expecting danger, and this makes them appear extremely cautious, especially in public settings. They may also start to engage in self-destructive behaviors, such as excessive drinking, excessive sex, and other addictions, which are merely attempting to drown their pain. They tend to have difficulties first getting asleep, and then having a quality sleep.

People living with PTSD have a hard time focusing on the task at hand as they become easily distracted by external stimuli. They tend to give exaggerated emotional and physical responses, giving them an appearance of emotional instability. Additionally, they experience intense feelings of shame and guilt, as they might blame themselves for the traumatic event. For instance, it is not uncommon for a woman who was raped to feel guilty and blame herself for making herself ripe for the ordeal.

Causes of PTSD

Considering that research into mental health conditions is

still at the early stage, there's no concrete evidence to point to the real cause of PTSD. But traditional knowledge indicates that distressing and traumatic events are largely behind PTSD.

- Painful events: you don't have to through them yourself. Even witnessing a painful event is enough to cause your PTSD. For instance, if you witnessed the loss of your loved one through a degenerative disease.

- Family affair: if your parents have had various mental illnesses, you are at risk of developing these illnesses yourself, and you might pass on this condition to your progeny as well.

- Environment: if you associate with people who have symptoms of PTSD, you may eventually ape their traits that eventually birth PTSD in you.

- Brain problems: if there's a disconnect between how your brain processes external stimuli and the responses it gives, it may result in chemical and hormone imbalances, resulting in PTSD.

Risk factors

Almost anyone can develop post-traumatic stress

disorder, but the following factors increase your probability of acquiring this illness.

• Lack of a support system: bad things happen all the time, but they shouldn't hold us hostage. If you have a good support system, you should get over the trauma and go back to being normal. However, if you have no support system, you might get crushed under the intense emotions and develop PTSD.

• Childhood abuse: for instance, being brought up by ruthless parents or getting sexually abused.

• Sensitive job: taking up a job that exposes you to the dark side of human life. For instance, military, police photographers, and surgeons.

• Mental health: if you are already battling other mental illnesses, you are more likely to develop PTSD.

• Unhealthy habits: you are also likely to develop PTSD if you have taken to unhealthy habits such as excessive drinking and binge eating.

Treating post-traumatic stress disorder (PTSD) with CBT

Step one: Identifying the symptoms

This initial step is critical because apart from helping a therapist understand the unique aspects of the illness bedeviling their patient. It is also a perfect time for them to bond, considering that the success of Cognitive Behavioral Therapy depends on the collaboration between the therapist and the patient. The following are some of the questions that the therapist will ask in order to have a better understanding of their patient's troubles:

- What runs through their minds when they remember a tragic event?
- What are their physical reactions to remembering a traumatic event?
- Do they experience invasive memories of the traumatic event?
- Do they experience nightmares related to specific traumatic events?
- To what extent have they lost interest in things they once enjoyed?
- How detached are you from other people?
- What activities, feelings, and thoughts have you been avoided since the trauma?

• Do you have any difficulty remembering any aspect of the trauma?

During this phase, the therapist expounds on what ails the patient and tries to make them understand how the trauma influences various aspects of their lives, and the actionable steps they may have to take in order to restore their life to normalcy.

They must also set achievable goals. The goals should guide the patient back into a healthy life where they are not affected by their traumatic past. The goals should be as specific as possible:

• Stop blaming myself or my spouse for the accident
• Start playing ping pong again
• Start embracing the people of the world instead of shunning them
• Start going out more
• Not run away from any reminders of the accident

Step two: explain the rationale of treatment

At this stage, the therapist is done selling the patient to CBT as the best treatment approach, but they may want to expound on how the treatment works. The therapist gets to explain how CBT addresses the deep-seated factors that influence PTSD and highlight types of people who are susceptible to this illness.

- Flexibility: the thing about CBT is that it is not rooted in some rigid set of rules. It is virtually a technique of self-exploration, except you have someone to watch over you and ensure that you don't falter. In order to come up with the most effective treatment, both the therapist and the patient must work together.

- Attitude: CBT not only cures you of your mental illness but helps a lot in terms of improving your attitude toward yourself and others. Studies show that a person's attitude is every bit as important as a person's qualifications for career advancement.

- Goal-setting: CBT allows you to have a multiple-thronged approach to your issues. You can achieve many goals by adhering to particular exercises.

Step three: understanding how your trauma caused PTSD

Some of the traumatic events that can lead to PTSD include:

- Fatal road accidents
- Sexual assault
- Mugging
- Miscarriage
- Domestic abuse
- Sexual abuse
- Witnessing violent deaths
- Terrorist attack victim
- Being taken, hostage
- Floods
- Degenerative diseases

When we experience trauma, the last thing on our mind is political correctness or critical thinking.

We can easily grab an incomplete thought and run with it. CBT helps us be objective so that we may have a clear idea of how the past affects our present conditions.

If besides experiencing something traumatic, you had also been suffering from depression and anxiety, you are at a much greater risk of developing full-blown PTSD.

The therapist helps you understand that PTSD comes about due to the following reasons:

• Survival mechanism: one school of thought says that PTSD is merely a biological response aimed at strengthening your survival capacity. For instance, the flashbacks are merely an attempt by the brain to get a clear glimpse of the details of the horrible event so that next time, you are more than prepared to prevent a repeat of the same. The feeling of being on edge is aimed at sharpening your reflexes.

• High adrenaline: when we are in stressful situations, the body secretes adrenaline to trigger quick action. Some people might not lose the ability to produce high levels of adrenaline, and it could lead to PTSD.

• Brain changes: if you have undergone significant brain changes, you may be unable to process external stimuli accurately, leading to false emotional responses, and eventually, PTSD.

Step four: developing positive thoughts

Once you learn of the various ways your mind is relying on inaccurate data to arrive at decisions, you can purpose to restructure your thoughts and eradicate PTSD.

• Cognitive restructuring: as a victim of a traumatic event, you might have become so shocked that you want nothing that reminds you of that experience. But that's the wrong approach. You should welcome the idea of being able to revisit your traumatic past and even talk about it. Once you demystify the trauma, you can move on quite easily.

• Play the script to the end: once you have undergone something traumatic, your body might make you feel on edge. This is a biological response aimed at preparing you more aware of your environment. Thus, you might find yourself scared of getting into specific areas or situations. In such instances, you ought to play the script to the end, so that you will find out nothing terrible will happen anyway.

• Muscle relaxation: once the anxieties and fears build

up inside of your mind, you can engage in progressive muscle relaxation in order to relieve yourself of these negative energies.

Step Five: Therapy Progress

As you keep practicing the exercises your therapist has assigned you; you will experience positive results. At this stage, you must start pushing the limits so that you may quicken your recovery.

Made in the USA
Middletown, DE
11 September 2020